Successful
SMALL GROUPS

FROM THEORY TO REALITY

KURT W. JOHNSON

Review and Herald® Publishing Association
www.ReviewandHerald.com
Since 1861

Published by Review and Herald® Publishing Association, Hagerstown, MD 21741-1119

This book was
Edited by Russell Holt
Copyedited by Judy Blodgett
Designed by: ChristianDsign.com
Cover image by: istockphoto.com
Typeset: 11/14 Bembo

PRINTED IN U.S.A.

15   14   13   12   11   5   4   3   2   1

Library of Congress Cataloging-in-Publication Data

Johnson, Kurt W., 1950-   .
    Successful small groups: from theory to reality / Kurt W. Johnson.
        p. cm.
    Includes bibliographical references.
1. Church group work. 2. Small groups—Religious aspects—Christianity. I. Title.
    BV652.2.J643 2011
    253'.7—dc22

                            2011001941

ISBN 978-0-8280-2561-4

CONTENTS

Also by Kurt W. Johnson:

Face to Face With Jesus (Bible Study Guide)
How to Give a Bible Study
LifeLine Bible Study Guides, Book 1
LifeLine Bible Study Guides, Book 2
Peace Is an Inside Job (Bible Study Guides)
Prayer Works
When Heaven Pauses

To order, call 1-800-765-6955.

Visit us at www.reviewandherald.com for information on other Review and Herald® products.

PREFACE

In the power of the Holy Spirit

This is a book about sharing your belief in God and the Bible with others through a small group. In this book we discuss methods—the how-to's of organizing and leading a small group. Let me make this disclaimer at the outset: methods and training are futile and of little value unless they are combined with a Spirit-filled life. The power that changes lives is *God's* power—not any power that comes from you or me.

Successful teaching methodologies are important—even necessary—but they do not replace the need to spend time in Bible study, prayer, and seeking the daily infilling of the Holy Spirit in your life. In fact, a Spirit-filled person with *no training* is more powerful than the most highly trained individual who does not have the Spirit of God in his or her life.

Should we conduct training events and share methodologies? Yes. Both Scripture and the Spirit of Prophecy give examples and counsel regarding the importance of training and following successful methods in soul winning. Ellen White wrote: "On such occasions as our annual camp meetings we must never lose sight of the opportunities afforded for teaching the believers how to do practical missionary work in the place where they may live. In many instances it would be well to set apart certain men to carry the burden of different lines of educational work at these meetings. Let some help the people to learn how to give Bible readings and to conduct cottage meetings. Let others bear the burden of teaching the people how to practice the principles of health and temperance, and how to give treatments to the sick. Still others may labor in the interests of our periodical and book work."[1]

But more important than anything else is seeking a Spirit-filled life. Jesus told His disciples, "John truly baptized with water, but you shall be baptized with the Holy Spirit not many days from now. . . . But you shall receive power when the Holy Spirit has come upon you; and you shall be witnesses to Me in Jerusalem, and in all Judea and Samaria, and to the end of the earth" (Acts 1:5-8).

"The Savior knew that no argument, however logical, would melt hard hearts or break through the crust of worldliness and selfishness. He knew that His disciples must receive the heavenly endowment; that the gospel would be effective only as it was proclaimed by hearts made warm and lips made eloquent by a living knowledge of Him who is the way, the truth, and the life."[2]

As you read this book on sharing Jesus Christ through small-group ministry, I encourage you to seek a daily, moment-by-moment relationship with Jesus Christ. Ask daily for the power of the Holy Spirit to fill your life continually and change you to be like Jesus, and use you mightily in leading people into a relationship with Him.

---

[1]Ellen G. White, *Testimonies for the Church*, vol. 9, pp. 82, 83.
[2]Ellen G. White, *The Acts of the Apostles*, p. 31.

INTRODUCTION

My small-group journey

My small-group journey began back in college—Walla Walla College (now Walla Walla University). I was off-campus outreach director. Flower children, Jesus people, beads, long hair, beards, peace, love, and anti-war slogans were culturally relevant. So we packed up our guitars, door flyers, and a Bible and headed to a nearby park. The strategy was simple: hand out flyers announcing a concert and group discussion at the park bandstand in one hour. At the appointed time we began with popular praise songs, and then I or one of my friends would give a brief talk to launch a discussion and invite those present to join a discussion with the various groups sitting around on the grass.

We came prepared with several questions to talk about. These were designed to "mine" the text and lead the groups into making the topic culturally relevant. That was the kicker—helping others to discuss the topic that Jesus and the gospel is worth considering. We had pamphlets, Voice of Prophecy "*Way-Out*" Bible lessons, and other helpful literature spread out on a blanket, free for the taking.

During my senior year in college my small-group experience became a bit more formal. I hopped aboard a DC-10 along with my mentor and professor, Malcom Maxwell, and fellow classmates for my first airplane flight. Our destination was Lincoln, Nebraska, and a collegiate witnessing rally. After the plane's wheels connected with the pavement and our meetings got under way, Pastor Jerry Brass, union youth director, along with other directors, led out in my first "formal" small-group training.

These two college experiences launched me into a lifelong experience in small groups. The settings varied: home prayer groups, Bible study groups, better living/health groups, and video discussion groups. Small groups were my early ministry experience, because the churches and communities I pastored were small. It was a built-in natural experience.

While serving as Sabbath school/personal ministries director in the Oregon Conference, I was part of a team that centered our conference witnessing strategy on small groups.

Our Oregon Conference team crisscrossed our conference with training events and rallies, equipping church members for small-group ministry and connecting with their friends and family.

During our launch period almost 800 small groups were started in our conference. These groups, titled "Homes of Hope," met around kitchen tables, in family rooms, places of business, even in a funeral home!

From that experience, our conference team birthed the North American Division small-group and prayer conferences, with attendees from around the world. Pastors and lay leaders spent an entire week together, singing, praying, meeting in workshops, processing, discussing, and becoming better equipped for small-group ministry.

Since then I have had the unique privilege of teaching small-group ministry cross-culturally and learning/growing from this interaction. From the villages of Borneo to Novosibirsk in the middle of Siberia, and the beautiful city of Sydney, and numerous other locations worldwide and across North America. I have been a member of a small group, mentored small-group leaders, and have written small-group books and Bible guides. Undergirding all this is my belief that small groups are a *way of life,* not a strategy or method.

Over the years I have experienced a cultural change in small-group strategies and methods. I have changed. My approach to small groups has broadened and adapted as society has changed. That is why I am writing this book—my third—on small groups. It is a part of my life journey, my ministry focus. Relevancy is fluid, and our small-group experience must be fluid if we want to reach today's masses. The biblical principles of small groups remain the same. The basic agenda never changes. But the way we approach and apply these principles is ever-changing. My prayer for you is that God will work through you mightily in ministry. That God will surprise you in what He accomplishes through your willingness to share about Him.

Getting started

The purpose of this book is threefold: to inspire, to equip, and to serve as a launching pad into small-group ministry. To accomplish this task, the book is divided into three sections:

Section I: Small-Group Basics. This section discusses the fundamental how-to's of organizing and leading a small group. For readers who like to "cut to the chase" and get going, this section will be their "bread and butter."

Section II: Small-Group Leadership. Dedicated, equipped leaders are fundamental to the success of any movement. Establishing a small-group movement in your church and community is no different. You will need sound leadership with a foundation anchored in God's vision for ministry. This section of the book will explore how to make this happen.

Section III: Digging Deeper. People are "wired" differently. Some are task-oriented—they don't have time to probe the history or digest the biblical and philosophical reasons behind small-group ministry. They simply want to get the job done. Others like to know what makes something function the way it does. What does God have to say about it? How does our Adventist heritage and literature assist in the process? This section will provide answers and some interesting stories to illustrate the historical and biblical foundations of small-group ministry.

Choose your section or read all three. Whatever you do, remember that through prayer, Bible study, and a dependence on God, you will experience a Spirit-filled life. No matter how timid or scared you may feel, God will use you with boldness in proclaiming the good news of the gospel.

God believes in you! God has gifted you! God has equipped you! God fills you with His Spirit! I believe in God's creative power, thus I believe in you—God makes no mistakes! So humbly trust God, and *you* through *Him* will change the world around you for the kingdom of Jesus Christ!

Enjoy the journey. Enjoy the read!

Kurt Johnson, D.Min.

SECTION I:
SMALL-GROUP BASICS

Chapter 1

FEEL THE FLAME

I was 4 years old when I first discovered that fire represents power.

I was alone in the living room. My mind was awhirl as I examined the room, trying to decide what to do next. I made my decision and headed for the electrical outlet on the wall beside my dad's chair. Now, this outlet was unusual looking—that was why it fascinated me. The outlets we used for the lamps were small (they carried 110 volts of electricity). But this outlet was large and had room for only one electrical plug, instead of the usual two. This electrical outlet was used for our 220-volt heater on cold winter days.

I examined the outlet with the curious fingers and eyes of a 4-year-old. *Why was this electrical outlet bigger than the others on the wall? Why did this outlet have three slots instead of two? Why did these slots go different directions?*

As I continued my investigation, I discovered a wire hairpin lying on the floor near the outlet. Like most 4-year-olds, I promptly picked up the hairpin and shoved it into the outlet.

To this day, the next two seconds are etched securely in my mind.

There was a loud explosion!

A ball of fire burst from the outlet!

I was thrown backward—and found myself lying on the floor scared, dazed, and with a blackened hand!

My mom came running from the other room—her face ashen and shocked. She scooped me up in her arms—and I don't recall what happened after that. My mind has blanked out the rest of the episode.

I felt the flame that day and realized that fire and power go together. We read about fire and spiritual power in Acts 2. "Suddenly there came a sound from heaven, as of a rushing mighty wind, and it filled the whole house where they were sitting. Then there appeared to them divided tongues, as of fire, and one sat upon each of them. And they were all filled with the Holy Spirit" (verses 2-4).

Acts 4, two chapters after this story of Pentecost, is one of my favorite chapters in the Bible. This chapter describes what happens when the Holy Spirit fills every crevice and corner of one's life. Acts 4 shows us Peter and John preaching and giving Bible studies. The religious leaders of their day—the Jewish rulers, elders, and scribes—were very upset about what these apostles were saying. They were annoyed by the enthusiastic response people were making to their message. So Annas, the high priest, and others of the ruling family called Peter and John in for a talk. "When they had set them in the midst, they asked, 'By what power or by what name have you done this?' " (Acts 4:7). Peter responded by giving a wonderful testimony.

Verse 13 tells us what happened as a result. "When they saw the boldness of Peter and John, and perceived that they were uneducated and untrained men, they marveled. And they realized that they had been with Jesus."

Still, these religious rulers ordered the apostles to quit teaching about Jesus. But Peter and John replied, "We cannot but speak the things which we have seen and heard" (verse 20).

Peter and John continued ministering in Jerusalem and praying with their fellow Christians. These are the words that came out of that prayer circle: "Now, Lord, look on their threats, and grant to Your servants that with all boldness they may speak Your word, by stretching out Your hand to heal, and that signs and wonders may be done through the name of Your holy Servant Jesus" (verses 29, 30).

I like what happened at the end of this session of prayer. Verse 31 states: "And when they had prayed, the place where they were assembled together was shaken; and they were all filled with the Holy Spirit, and they spoke the word of God with boldness."

Remember, these disciples were not ordained preachers; they were fisherman, laborers, tax collectors—in other words, they were people just like you and me. They loved Jesus. They wanted to tell others about Him. They too were scared, nervous, and unsure of themselves. The disciples had once even hidden in an upper room from fear of the authorities. But through prayer and relying on the Holy Spirit, they allowed God to use them mightily in His service!

God wants to use you in ministry. He wants to give you a vision of ministry through a small group. You see, the disciples were part of a movement—a Spirit-led movement. God had put His vision for them into their minds and hearts. After Pentecost their desire was to "go, dear Father, where You want me to go. To do, dear Father, what You want me to do."

I like the way Oswald Chambers describes vision in his book *My Utmost for His Highest:* "God gives us the vision, then He takes us down to the valley to batter us into the shape of the vision, and it is in the valley that so many of us faint and give way. Every vision will be made real if we will have patience."[1]

You see, a vision is something that works *on* our lives and *in* our lives; it is not something we work on. No one ever attains the vision, but we live in the inspiration of it until God accomplishes it in us. Vision is a passion, a calling, a drive, or compulsion that simply will not let us go. We talk about the need to "catch the vision." But the type of vision that God wants us to have is not caught; it catches us.[2]

Vision alters us. One cannot remain the same while gripped by a vision. It is impossible! When we are changed by God, we are no longer concerned about our vision, but we wait for God to shape us to fill our part of His vision. Being part of God's vision can be costly—Jesus told us that it may cost us family, friends, houses, and lands—even our freedom.

In fact, if the vision is unclear and we have not been altered and shaped by the Spirit to fit God's vision, we will find that the cost of following God's vision will be too high. When life gets tough, those whose vision is built on shifting sand will bail out of the boat.[3]

But that is where God steps into the picture. God says to you and to me, "I will put My Spirit in you, and you shall live, and I will place you in your own land. Then you shall know that I, the Lord, have spoken it and performed it" (Eze. 37:14). Notice the emphasis on God's initiative. God has a vision of His church—you and me—in partnership with Him.

God says to you and me, "Go to your friends and neighbors, your work associates. Go—and I will make you fishers of men. I will speak through you with boldness! Go! I am with you until the end of the world." This includes you starting a small group and inviting some of your unchurched friends to participate. This book describes the steps you need to take. Are you ready? Let's get started!

---

[1] Oswald Chambers, *My Utmost for His Highest,* July 6.

[2] William Beckham, *The Second Reformation,* p. 23.

[3] *Ibid.,* p. 21.

Chapter 2

HERE I AM, READY OR NOT!

I was 41 years old when I learned to snowplow. I thought I blended in real well with the 10-year-olds in the beginning ski class on Oregon's Mount Hood. In fact, after the verbal-instructions quiz I was the top student in the class—until I put on the skis! I learned with amazement that if someone gently bumps you, the skis actually move by themselves and go right over the top of screaming, angry 10-year-olds—with you attached!

I soon figured out that I wasn't wanted. I'm not sure if it was the stares of a half dozen kids or the fact that the instructor moved me into the class for "older people" that made me catch on. But it wasn't long until I and a group of Johnny-come-lately skiers followed our instructor, Peter, down the beginner's run. I still remember him taking us to the top of a hill that he called an "intermediate" run. I peered over the edge and immediately christened him "Kamikaze Pete." "You've got to be kidding!" I protested.

Kamikaze Pete looked at me with a silly grin and said, "You can do it! Just push yourself over the edge and snowplow if you need to—right?"

Kamikaze Pete taught us several things. We stayed together as a group. We encouraged each other. We helped each other up if we fell. We even chased each other's loose skis down the hill. We were taught to let each other lean on our shoulders in order to reattach the boot to the ski. We went at a pace that allowed all of us to succeed. We cheered for each other. We learned to say "I'm sorry" when we accidentally ran into a ski mate. And when we graduated to the next level, there were hugs, smiles, and congratulations. We had made it—together!

My ski class, including Kamikaze Pete, was what a small group is all about. I am sure the 10-year-olds were pleased when I moved on to those my own age. But they wished me no harm—well, I hope not! But when I walked, stumbled, skied into their world, the unstated watchword was— "Here I Am, Ready or Not!"

That is really like everyday life. We don't choose everyone that we become mixed together with. But we learn to get along and live life together—and sometimes, as the Bible says, we become a friend who sticks closer than a brother or sister (see Prov. 18:24). That is how God planned it.

In the beginning—and even now—God's plan is that we live a life that is like His. He wants us to be loving, accepting, forgiving people. Sometimes we don't do that very well, do we? We mutter at the person who cuts us off on the road. We yell at the dog, or worse yet, at the members of our family. It's hard, when you are tired and frazzled, to always live like Jesus.

Before God created the first man and woman, He said, "Let Us make man in Our image" (Gen. 1:26). God wasn't saying that He was going to make a lot of "little gods" just like Him. No. One key meaning of "image" is that we would resemble Him in the way we live and treat each other.

Humanity did not do a very good job of following God's plan. Compare God and us. The Bible describes God this way: kind, just, fair, loving, forgiving, putting others first, meeting the needs of others, providing healing, dying for us, wanting us to be with Him forever.

Our biblical relatives struggled just as you and I have. Cain murdered his brother; Moses and his brother and sister got into a big fight; Job's friends turned against him; Jacob deceived his brother; David had an affair; Jesus' disciples fought over positions in ministry; the rich young ruler did not want to share his money; James and John wanted to burn down a city; and Paul, Barnabas, and John Mark had to figure out how to get along—just to name a few of the issues that came up among our spiritual family members.

God did not give up on us, however. Before Jesus returned to heaven, He prayed to God the Father and asked Him for something for us. Listen to this profound request: "That they may be one as We are" (John 17:11). Later in His prayer Jesus makes this request even more intense: "That they all may be one, as You, Father, are in Me, and I in You; that they also may be one in Us, that the world may believe that You sent Me" (verse 21).

Being one

What was this oneness for which Jesus prayed? It was not a oneness—a unity—of organization, administration, or obtaining unanimous votes at your board meeting, although that is OK too. *Rather, it was a unity of personal relationship.* The union between Jesus and His Father was one of love and working together. As Jesus went on to say in His prayer: "That the love with which You loved Me may be in them, and I in them" (verse 26).

This love, this "getting along," can tear down barriers that people have erected between each other. As Jesus saw it and prayed for it, this unity was to convince the world that He and Christianity were for real. That there is nothing fake about Him! This is important. Why? *Because it is more natural for people to be divided than united. It is more natural for people to "fly apart" than to "come together."* Real unity between Christians is truly a "God thing," not a "man thing."[1] Jesus' prayer shows that He thinks it is possible for us to have this type of unity—to get along. In fact, Jesus spent three years modeling community, family—oneness—to His disciples. Jesus had poured His life into this motley group of misfits because He firmly believed they could live together in "oneness."

This prayer for oneness comes at the end of Jesus' life on this earth—just before He faced the Garden of Gethsemane and the cross. If Jesus had asked His disciples for their final prayer requests before He headed back to heaven, I don't imagine they would have included oneness. It's more likely that their list would have included kicking the Romans out of Judea, a new fishing boat, or a retirement home on the Sea of Galilee.[2]

Jesus' prayer for oneness didn't end with the original twelve disciples. He prayed for unity for every person who goes by the name of Christian! That's right, no one is left out. Listen to His words: "I do not pray for these [His twelve disciples] alone, but also for those who will believe in Me through their word; that they all may be one" (verses 20, 21).

Belonging

Oneness was important to Jesus, because when there is "oneness" among us, it means we belong to Him and to each other. That is His plan for every person ever born on Planet Earth.

We all have a fundamental need, which in simple terms is *belonging.* Belonging overrides a lot of items we use to try to make religion and church attractive. We use PowerPoint presentations to illustrate our sermons, track lighting to brighten our stage, music teams to guide our worship, and the latest electronic gadgets to keep people's attention. That's all good; we should use every new method possible to introduce people to Jesus as the one who can meet their daily needs. However, all of our innovative worship ideas and technology will never replace the one simple item that will keep people coming back to church again and again—*knowing that they belong.* You can have the most innovative and creative worship service possible, and if a person does not feel wanted and accepted, they will go where they *are* accepted and where people care that they exist—even if that accepting place is a run-down storefront with a screechy sound system.

"Belonging" is simply a close-knit group of friends that doesn't feel complete if someone in the group is missing. Keeping our terminology simple, that is what a small group is all about. A small group is a group of people who truly become friends—friends who are there for each other whether they are sad, happy, discouraged, celebrating, or mourning. Friends who pray with you, challenge you, hold you accountable, laugh with you, and love you no matter what you do or where your past has taken you. Together, by God's grace and power, they live out the phrase "We wish to see Jesus" (John 12:21) in the way we treat each other.

Once we become one with Jesus, then we are to become one with each other. In fact, the Bible talks about what it means to live a life of oneness with each other. Some call these verses the "one-another passages." I have never counted them, but those who have say there are more than 50 such verses. Here are a few of them:

- "Confess your trespasses to one another, and pray for one another, that you may be healed" (James 5:16).
- "Through love serve one another" (Gal. 5:13).
- "Bear one another's burdens, and so fulfill the law of Christ" (Gal. 6:2).
- "Be kind to one another, tenderhearted, forgiving one another, just as God in Christ also forgave you" (Eph. 4:32).
- "Bearing with one another, and forgiving one another, if anyone has a complaint against another; even as Christ forgave you" (Col. 3:13).

As we read these verses, it becomes obvious that an inspiring worship service and a monthly potluck aren't enough to make sure everyone "belongs." At least it wasn't for Cheryl, as we will see in the next chapter.

---

[1] William Barclay, *The Gospel of John*, vol. 2, pp. 217, 218.
[2] See Bill Donahue and Russ Robinson, *Building a Church of Small Groups*.

Chapter 3

WHY CHERYL WASN'T MISSED

Her words still haunt me: "I didn't fit in." "I'm not sure I belonged." "People probably cared, but it just didn't work out." Those were the phrases Cheryl, a new Christian, used to explain why she was no longer attending church after only one year. The reason had nothing to do with Bible doctrines, questions over new beliefs, or pressure from relatives. It had everything to do with the need to belong.

I remember the day I baptized Cheryl. She had attended an evangelistic reaping series and continued with Bible studies and attendance at church socials and worship. Alice, one of the "over 60 years of age" members of the church, took Cheryl, a 22-year-old, under her care. Alice was there beside Cheryl at every event, making sure she was not alone and introducing her to others. Eventually Cheryl was introduced to the young adults closer to her age. People were friendly, but close relationships just never happened. Cheryl wasn't invited to be part of anyone's life outside of the church meetings. Gradually she sensed she "didn't belong." It was several weeks before someone said, "Hey, where's Cheryl? I haven't seen her lately, have you?"

A place to belong

What Cheryl was looking for was relationships—a place to *belong*. We sometimes call this need by the formal word, "community." Community is usually associated with geography (a neighborhood or a city), sociology (one's network of relatives), political groups (national, state, or local), or sometimes a support group (grief, divorce, addictions, etc.).

Cheryl needed a small group!

Community refers to a group of people who have common goals in their personal lives and who have come together to form a supportive friendship with one another. The bottom line is that in order to be physically, socially, mentally, and spiritually healthy, we all need one another, and we need God. I believe that a small group is one of the best places to live out this lifestyle.

To be "doing church" right, your church must have intentional community life.

Simply stated, Christian community is living like Jesus in our relationships with one another—being caring, loving, accepting, forgiving, understanding, and patient. That is, being available for each other in both the good times of life and the difficult times—watching out for each other.

My neighbor Sam demonstrated community to me last Thanksgiving. At the end of summer I turn off the water line that goes from my house to the garden and drain the pipe so that it won't freeze during the winter. But that summer I forgot. While I was visiting my son for the Thanksgiving holiday—seven hours away from home—the sprinkler riser froze one night and broke. Later that day a geyser of water was shooting two feet into the air. Since I wasn't planning to be home for a few days, the water would have poured out of the pipe nonstop—except for Sam.

Sam noticed the problem. He shut off the main valve to stop the water from pouring out. Now, if that was all Sam had done, I would have been grateful. However, he drove to the local hardware store and purchased fittings to fix the broken sprinkler. Then he repaired the pipe. And a few days later, when the weather warmed up, he turned the water back on.

When I thanked Sam for taking care of my needs, he just grinned from ear to ear and said, "No problem. That's what friends are for!"

This is community in action! This is how God wants us to live our faith.

God embodies community. The Father, Son, and Holy Spirit are one—there is unity, cooperation, teamwork, and a love for one another among the three members of the Godhead. It was because of their special relationship that they decided to express that love by creating human beings in their likeness to experience and enjoy the same relationship.

During the creation of the world God said, "Let Us make man in Our image, according to Our likeness" (Gen. 1:26). We read next that God said, "It is not good that man should be alone; I will make him a helper comparable to him" (Gen. 2:18).

God desires us to find community in relationships. God made men and women to have positive, supportive relationships with one another. It is unnatural to be out of harmony with God and one another. Whether married or single, we all need each other, and we all need God.

God made us to belong. People are searching for a place to belong. As God's people, let's meet that need! Let's not live in isolation (see John 17:20-23).

Alone against the world

Too many Christians live like the character in the old television show *The Lone Ranger.* The Lone Ranger always appeared on the scene at the appropriate moment to solve the dilemma. No one knew who the Lone Ranger was in everyday life. He seemed to need no one (besides Tonto) and faced life all alone. Whenever there was a crisis, he was there, and then—*poof*—he rode off into the sunset.

That is how some Christians live. They hide away from one another except for Sabbath. The rest of the week they are wrapped up in jobs, household duties, a church meeting once in a while, hobbies/interests, and their own group of friends. They rarely have time for prayer meeting, a weekly small group, individual Bible studies, friendship evangelism, or other ministries. Periodically, when an announcement is made in church about an emergency need, they drop everything and help, only to retreat back into their own cocoon once the crisis has passed.

Living in isolation is a far cry from God's plan for individual uniqueness in the context of community. In 1 Corinthians 12 the apostle Paul compares the church to the human body; he points out that every person has a unique role in the church, just as each part of the body has a special function. Each unique gift is needed and necessary. And if one person suffers, the entire church community suffers, just as the whole body suffers if a single part is hurting.

It is in community that we are most challenged to grow up in Jesus. We don't lose our uniqueness in community; we find it. We are most uniquely ourselves when we are with others who need us to complement the mutual picture of God that we are creating. Together we become what we could not become alone. This is God's plan for His church.

The apostle Paul said it well in 2 Corinthians 5:15: "He [Christ] died for all, that those who live should live no longer for themselves, but for Him who died for them and rose again."

When one is connected to Jesus, self becomes secondary, and others become primary. "Christianity builds no walls of separation between man and his fellow man, but binds human beings to God and to one another."[1]

Isn't this the goal of the church and Christianity—living in a unity and harmony that becomes an avenue for the outpouring of the latter rain of the Holy Spirit greater than what was seen at Pentecost?[2]

I was conducting a training seminar on how to deal with conflict within small groups. After the meeting Jennifer, one of the group leaders, pointed to another small-group leader, Sarah, and told me this story. When Sarah first began coming to the group, she had nothing positive to add to it; instead, she subtracted from it. Sarah was like a puppy that had been beaten. She wouldn't look anyone in the eye; she sat with her head down; her comments were always negative. But the group praised her good qualities and made her feel accepted and needed. It wasn't long until Sarah began to blossom. "Now look at her!" Jennifer exclaimed. Together we stood and watched a vivacious young woman laugh, smile, and hug her fellow group leaders. Sarah was now giving others what she had been given. She had received the Holy Spirit in a relationship with caring Christians.

I believe that one of the best and most natural ways to create a caring church is through small groups.

---

[1] See Ellen G. White, *Gospel Workers*, p. 140.
[2] Julie A. Gorman, "Close Encounters—The Real Thing," *Christian Educational Journal* 13, no. 3.

Chapter 4

THE BIBLE AND SMALL GROUPS

The church sanctuary was bursting at the seams with people. I was amazed! I had never seen so many people come out for a seminar on the topic "sharing your faith with others." Unbelievable! The attendees carefully followed my presentation that afternoon, listening intently. At the end, questions began to flow. "Does this 'new' method of small groups come from the Bible or from some other book I've read?" I soon discovered that some had come to the seminar, not because they wanted to learn how to share Jesus through a Bible study in their home, but because they wanted to analyze this "new" method of outreach being proposed for local church members. They had never shared Jesus and Scripture this way before!

However, a little research on their part would have revealed that although home small groups may have been new to them, such groups were not new to God or to their Adventist forebears. In fact, the Bible, the history of the early church, and our own Adventist heritage bear this out. Later chapters will deal with the history, but for now let's look at a biblical basis for small-group ministry.

Old Testament principles

The principles of small-group ministry can be traced to the first verse in the Old Testament—Genesis 1:1. "In the beginning God created the heavens and the earth." The Hebrew word translated "God" in this verse is plural, indicating that more than one divine Person was involved in Creation. Christian belief holds that the members of the Godhead, the Father, Son, and Holy Spirit, are one in purpose and design—a small group, if you please.

After the human race was created in God's image and likeness (see Gen. 1:27), God said something that provides a rationale for small groups. He said, "It is not good that man should be alone" (Gen. 2:18). Men and women were created as social creatures; they live happier, more productive lives in groups. The family unit was instituted to fulfill basic human needs. Just as a newborn baby needs the love and attention of a family for healthy development, so a newborn child of God needs the nurture that only a small attentive group from the larger church family can provide. Genesis 2:18 does not mean that everyone has to be married to find fulfillment in life, but it does imply that we humans need each other socially.

Studies have shown the overwhelming importance of human touch to our emotional and physical well-being. Research on children's orphanages in England during World War II revealed that without human touch, children became morose and often died despite adequate nutrition and proper hygiene.

In the 1940s Dr. Fritz Talbot visited a children's clinic in Düsseldorf, Germany. The wards were neat and tidy, but something caught his attention. He noticed a old, rather plump woman carrying a sickly looking baby on her hip. He asked the medical director who the woman was and why she was carrying the child as she went about her duties. "She's 'Old Anna,'" the director replied. "When we have exhausted all medical possibilities for a baby, we give it to her to hold and stroke. She always seems to be successful in saving its life."

This observation and others led to major changes in the way some orphanages were run. Bellevue Hospital in New York City instituted a new policy: every baby was to be picked up, held, touched, and mothered several times a day. As a result, the death rate for infants there plummeted to fewer than 10 percent. A vital human need had been discovered—the need to be touched.*

Why do we need each other? Because it is God's plan.

When God created the first man and woman in Eden, He formed a small community in relationship to Himself. They walked together "in the cool of the day" (Gen. 3:8). Next God gave the man and woman a task to do together with Him. They were to tend the garden (see Gen. 2:15). They were also told to be fruitful and multiply (see Gen. 1:28), increasing the size of their group.

Here we see several key principles of group life. A small group is a minimum of three individuals—two humans and God. They interact and do things together. They want others to join their group and add to their social and spiritual development.

As the first created couple, Adam and Eve also formed a household and gave birth to all people and nations that followed. Because of sin, God's plan of community and harmony was periodically disrupted, as, for example, by the dispute between Cain and Abel and also at the Tower of Babel. But God proposed to bring restoration to these fractured relationships. He provided a solution for all humanity through Jesus Christ, and we are part of God's long-term plan for communicating this solution.

God, Moses, and Jethro

God's organizational structure for Israel involved large-, medium-, and small-group relationships. The nation was composed of groups and subgroups of various sizes; the nation was divided into tribes, which were divided into clans, which were divided into families and individual households. In the same manner spiritual Israel, God's church today, needs to have competent and balanced leadership at each level of the organizational structure. If the church overlooks any of these groupings, it will suffer in its mission.

The Old Testament concept of organizing from large to small is also seen in the leadership advice that Jethro, Moses' father-in-law, gave him while the Israelites were wandering in the desert. Pastor Moses had a church membership of more than 2 million. Exodus 38:26 states that the church in the wilderness was comprised of 603,550 men. Adding a wife and several children to each couple makes for a large congregation! It was no wonder Moses pulled his pastoral hair and said, "How can I alone bear your problems and your burdens and your complaints?" (Deut. 1:12). It is obvious that the task facing Moses was impossible. Many pastors today attempt to minister to a congregation with very little assistance. Yet it is impossible for pastors alone to meet the needs of all their members. That is one reason it is important for all the members to assist in ministry.

According to Exodus 18:21-23 Jethro told Moses to select able men who feared God, men of truth who were not greedy, and place them over the people. He instructed Moses to divide the people into groups of thousands, hundreds, fifties, and tens. This would mean that Moses needed approximately 60,000 leaders of ten, 12,000 leaders of fifty, 6,000 leaders of a hundred, and 600 leaders of a thousand—for a total of 78,600 leaders. Selecting the leaders and writing job descriptions for each must have been quite a task in itself. But God inspired Moses to follow these orders explicitly.

Sometimes pastors and lay leaders say it is not practical, necessary, or possible to organize a church into small groups. But Moses did! His smallest group was a unit of 10 people with a leader—the subject of this book!

Think about what occurred when Moses, and later Joshua, followed God's organizational structure. It led them to the Promised Land of Canaan. This was good, but God wanted them to occupy the land completely. Unfortunately, the Israelites quit before their mission was accomplished. They became complacent and didn't complete the task of winning Canaan completely for God.

Sometimes churches today do the same. Once they establish themselves in a community and attain a certain size, the members become complacent. They think that they are large enough already and that if they get too big, they will become impersonal. And they have many other excuses. But the mission of the church is not accomplished until Jesus returns. Jesus said to go into the entire world, to every race, tribe, and people. It is not enough simply to be present in a community; we must "occupy." We must organize the church for service. And group ministry is a part of God's plan.

Jesus and small groups

When Jesus was ready to found the Christian church, He began with a small group. Matthew 4:18-22 and Luke 6:13-16 list the 12 disciples Jesus chose. They needed some rough edges of character sanded off, but they were the beginning of Christianity.

Twelve is an interesting number. Sociologists tell us that once a group becomes larger than 12, the dynamic changes, and it is no longer a small group, but a midsize group. That is why it is often suggested for a small group to divide once it reaches approximately 12 members. If it doesn't, its survival rate is not good, because the small-group dynamic is no longer present. However, some groups deal with this issue by meeting as a larger group, and then dividing into smaller units that meet throughout the house for discussion and interaction.

Another interesting small-group phenomenon occurred within the unit of the 12 disciples. Jesus and the other disciples had close friends among

themselves. Jesus had a special closeness to Peter, James, and John. In the
Garden of Gethsemane Jesus asked these three to pray with Him, while the
other disciples were left in another part of the garden (see Matt. 26). Likewise, these three were singled out when on the Mount of Transfiguration
(see Matt. 17:1-3). There is nothing wrong with group members bonding with one another; this is quite natural. Encouraging close friendships
and prayer partnerships among the various members will assist the group
members in ministering to one another and will strengthen your group. In
addition, when it is time to form new groups, encourage the members to
form new groups/divide their existing groups according to their friendships. Friends working together and supporting each other makes for a
strong leadership team.

This is not how small-group multiplication used to be taught. It was a
beautiful sunny afternoon in southern California. I was attending a small-
group training event, but was fighting the desire to head to the white sands
of Malibu Beach! Beating off the temptation, I listened carefully as our instructor gave us specific instructions about how to divide and begin a new
group. It was almost a scientific formula—cold and impersonal. It was like
a recipe. 1. You train an assistant leader who becomes the new group leader.
2. The group leaders discuss who should be in each group. 3. Then the leaders try to convince the individuals to join the new groups according to the
leader's wishes. Back then it sounded logical; today it sounds illogical. Jesus
modeled the correct way all along—form new groups naturally, according
to how the Holy Spirit puts people together!

Small group versus large group

Which is more important, small-group or large-group time? The answer is
that small groups and large groups should not compete. The church needs
both. This is especially true in evangelism when small groups and evangelistic reaping meetings are combined to provide nurture and reaping. When
the newly baptized and those still seeking Jesus are placed in groups, there
is weekly accountability and a ready-made family to assist in the spiritual
growth of the individual. Jesus spent time with the multitudes, time with
the individual, and time in homes. He visited the home of Simon the leper;
He spent time with the woman at the well; He had an encounter with

Zacchaeus. Scripture says that when He saw the multitudes, He was moved with compassion for them. Small-group and large-group time is like faith and works—the two cannot be separated.

Jesus spent time with His small group, the disciples. He bonded with them, instructed them, prayed with them, and then took them with Him to observe how He ministered to others. Afterward, they retreated into their small group and debriefed and processed their ministry and mission (see Matt. 14:13-23; Mark 3:7). A casual reading of the Gospels reveals that Jesus spent more time one on one or in small-group settings than He did in large-group settings. Why? Because people are saved as individuals, not as a multitude.

Jesus always put people before structure and traditions. *His goal was redemptive relationships.* He told the disciples that if someone wants to be a leader in His organization, they must put others before themselves. A leader must be willing to serve others and give up selfish goals and desires (see Luke 22:24-30). In addition, Jesus told the religious leaders that their priority should be living the principles of the kingdom—not policing the rules of the kingdom. He said that it's what is on the inside of a person that counts, not the outward appearance (see Luke 17:20, 21). Once the relationship is correct, obedience will follow. In everything the church does, including small groups, people must be the number one priority. Members should not participate in group life to "fix" one another. It is the role of the Holy Spirit to convict and change lives. The members are to learn and live Scripture and support and pray for one another.

Jesus also used the small-group setting with His disciples *to train them for service.* It was a safe environment in which to share concerns and questions and to be able to grow from the experience. An example is the parable of the sower in Luke 8. The disciples were sitting with the crowd, listening to Jesus share the story and its application to life and ministry. When the disciples were alone with Jesus, they asked Him to explain the parable to them. I am sure the discussion helped in their understanding of how to share their faith in ways to assist people in accepting Jesus as Savior. Similarly, the small-group environment provides opportunities for each member to minister to the others in the group, invite their friends and relatives, and learn ministry in a nonthreatening setting.

Jesus used the small-group setting not only for sharing spiritual lessons, but as an environment in which to model leadership. The disciples were jealous of one another and fought with each other about who would be first in the kingdom. He was able to explain to them that the gifts of each person were to work in harmony with those of others under the guidance of the Holy Spirit (see Luke 22:24-30; Matt. 18:1-5).

Home-based small groups were important to Jesus in the formation, development, and success of the Christian church. Often His ministry occurred in the context of a home. "Then Jesus . . . went into the house. And His disciples came to Him" (Matt. 13:36). And while in the house He taught them. "He went to the Pharisee's house, and sat down to eat" (Luke 7:36). Then He proceeded to teach Simon about forgiveness. In short, Jesus began the Christian church and His ministry to the world through a small group. His example should speak volumes to His church today.

Small groups in the book of Acts

After Jesus' death, and after they had received the Holy Spirit at Pentecost, His followers began to live out these small-group principles that Jesus had modeled. In fact, the foundation of small groups and the agenda followed by a small group is based on Acts 2 and the believers' experience at Pentecost.

What does this scriptural foundation for small groups look like? The roots are found in the Spirit-filled church described in Acts 2. This chapter is must reading for an understanding of Spirit-filled church life. Here's a summary of the background of Acts 2.

Jesus told His disciples:

- He was going to return to heaven (see John 13:33).
- He would not leave them alone, but would give them the Holy Spirit (see John 14:15-18).
- The Holy Spirit would be their helper. He would teach them and help them remember what Jesus had taught them (see John 14:26).

Jesus assured the disciples that it was actually to their advantage that He return to heaven. The Holy Spirit, whom Jesus would send, would convict the world of sin, of right living, and of the need to make a decision for Jesus (see John 16:7-15).

After His resurrection, just before He returned to heaven, Jesus gave the disciples what we have come to call the Great Commission. He told the disciples, and all Christians, to go into all nations and make disciples, baptize them, and teach them to follow His teachings faithfully—guiding the believers in living the Christian life (see Matt. 28:18-20). Jesus then told the disciples to wait in Jerusalem for the Holy Spirit to come upon them (see Acts 1:4). When that happened, they would, He said, receive power and be His witnesses all over the world (see Acts 1:8).

Acts 2 describes the disciples receiving the power of the Holy Spirit. What then follows is a description of what a Spirit-filled church looks like. In verses 22-36 Peter preaches to the people about the fact that Jesus is the Messiah, the Savior of the world and the Son of God. After hearing the sermon, the people cried out, "What shall we do?" (verse 37). Peter told them to repent and be baptized for the forgiveness of their sins, and 3,000 people responded to his call and were baptized (see verses 38-41).

Then Acts 2 describes what church life was like for these newly baptized members of the newly formed, relatively pristine, Spirit-filled church. Verse 42 describes four items that were part of their daily church life:

- *First,* the believers devoted themselves to the apostles' teachings. Today we would call this Bible study.
- *Second,* there was fellowship with one another—love, caring, sharing, and nurture.
- *Third,* they broke bread together. That is, they ate together, and shared the emblems of the Lord's Supper together.
- *Fourth,* they prayed together.

Verse 43 adds a *fifth* element. It says that miracles and supernatural signs occurred in the church. Other Bible references mention conversions, healings, and even resurrections from the dead.

Verses 44 and 45 add a *sixth* dimension. These verses tell us that the believers had "all things in common" (verse 44) and sold their possessions in order to give freely to anyone in need. No doubt, some believers had lost their possessions when they had become Christians. New Christians sometimes found themselves without a job, money, or a home. Thus the members of the church helped one another and met the personal needs of the members. Today those needs might include financial help with food, housing, utilities, or medical bills. In addition, meeting needs might include alcohol and drug rehabilitation and recovery programs for other addictive habits. The focus is on the impact that Christians had and still have on the world around them—bettering the lives of the suffering, the poor, and others with similar needs.

Verse 46 states that the members met in the "temple" (large meetings of corporate worship) as well as "house to house" (small home meetings) and that "the Lord added to the church daily those who were being saved" (verse 47).

The mass meetings and the home meetings not only provided support, fellowship, and social life; they also were settings in which soul winning occurred—people were baptized. Some say that the purpose of small groups is to meet social needs. That is true. But the biblical model in Acts 2 also produces decisions for Jesus Christ! *If your small group is not reaching out to the unchurched as part of its format, then your group is not following the God-given principles found in Acts 2.*

Acts 2 provides your small-group agenda

Thus Acts 2:41-47 provides the agenda of activities for all of church life. Group life arises from these core elements. Let's apply the principles of Acts 2 to a small-group meeting. The items listed are:

Acts 2	Group Format
apostles' doctrine	Bible study
fellowship	personal sharing, social interaction, friendship
prayer	prayer time
breaking bread together	worshipping, eating together
all things in common	meeting personal needs of group members
people baptized	outreach and mission

The above ingredients are what make up the agenda of a small group.

A question that is sometimes asked by my seminar attendees at this point is: "How do small groups that are not Bible study groups fit into this format?" Some would argue that a small group must include all of the above items in order to really be a small group—to be "pure" or "wholistic" or "biblical." Others would argue that if a small group contains just one of these characteristics, it is a small group that meets the principles and agenda of Acts 2. We will discuss this in a later chapter, but for now, let's deal with the issue at hand—*that small groups are biblically based and have their foundation firmly rooted in Scripture.*

Based on this scriptural premise, we will now look at organizing and leading a home Bible study small group that includes all of the principles found in Acts 2:41, 42 mentioned in this chapter. Some call this type of group a wholistic small group. I will call it simply a Bible study group.

Once we finish discussing Bible study groups, we will consider other models of small groups and how they function.

Small group basics—let's get started . . .

---

*See www.uncommon-knowledge.co.uk/touch/touch-1.html.

Chapter 5

SMALL GROUPS 101—THE BASICS

A young woman approached me as I was conducting a small-group training seminar and said, "I hope this is a basic course for beginners, because I need lots of help! Please explain what a small group is." You may be wondering the same thing, so let's tackle that question first: What is a small group?

Definition of a small group

There are various definitions of a small group. Here are several examples:

A cell is a small group with an ideal size of eight to 15 people who meet together on a regular basis for worship, Bible study, outreach, discipleship, and prayer.[1] ("Cell" or "cell group" is a term some use for a small group.)

A small group within the church is a voluntary, intentional gathering of three to 12 people regularly meeting together with the shared goal of mutual Christian edification and fellowship.[2]

A small group is an intentional, face-to-face gathering of three to 12 people, on a regular time schedule, with the common purpose of discovering and growing in the abundant life of Christ.[3]

Some of these definitions ignore the important element of outreach. In fact, I have attended nationwide small-group training events in which nurture was seen as the only purpose for small groups, while outreach was ignored. This is a serious error. As we have already seen, Acts 2 specifies outreach as an essential part of the early Christians' house-to-house activities—followed by new accessions to the faith. Ellen White also states that small groups are for both outreach and nurture:

"The formation of small companies as a basis of Christian effort is a plan that has been presented before me by One who cannot err. If there is a large number in the church, let the members be formed into small companies, to work not only for the church members but for unbelievers also."[4]

The following definition is my own. It incorporates all the necessary elements that I believe are involved in a small group:

A small group is an intentional, face-to-face gathering of three to 12 people, meeting on a regular schedule, with the common purpose of developing relationships, meeting felt needs of group members, growing spiritually, and laying plans to lead others to accept Jesus as Lord and Savior of their lives.

Four core relationships

The definition of a small group must grow out of the core purpose of a small-group meeting—which is to develop and build community. And "community" is another way to say "relationships." The following four relationships are key to a successful small group:

1. *The God-to-person relationship.* The group should focus on what God wants to happen to the members individually and be sensitive to His touch in their lives.

2. *The person-to-God relationship.* Individual response to the moving of God's Spirit is a primary part of group life. Group members must be aware of the Holy Spirit touching the lives of group members so they can be supportive. As the Spirit impresses members to respond, ordinary people will do extraordinary things for God.

3. *The person-to-person relationship.* The response of members to God will affect the way they relate to one another. As they grow in the Spirit, they will be supportive of one another, pray for one another, assist with personal needs, be more understanding and forgiving, and desire for others to have the same experience.

4. *The person-to-world relationship.* A group cannot be spiritually whole and not reach out to others beyond the circle. God has called people to gather together, but He has also told them to go into all the world. God calls for groups to help fulfill this commission. Group leaders must model outreach. This is one critical factor in the success of a small group.

Group life arises from these core relationships. As we saw in the previous chapter, Acts 2 provides the agenda of activities for all of church life. Let's review, again, the principles outlined in Acts 2:41-47 as they relate to a small-group meeting:

Acts 2	Group Format
apostles' doctrine	Bible study
fellowship	personal sharing, social interaction
prayer	prayer time
breaking bread together	worshipping, eating together
all things in common	meeting personal needs of group members
people baptized	outreach and mission

Based on this outline, all small groups will have five common components: loving, learning, deciding, doing, and praying. *Loving* involves listening and sharing one's personal story. *Learning* comes by studying the Bible and gaining knowledge of God's will and His truth. *Deciding* involves making group decisions about what to do with the children, what the group will do with their time together, when to multiply the group, and other such matters. Much of the deciding is done in the initial meetings and is not a major ongoing focus of the group. *Doing* is the mission of the group. What is its purpose? What is the group trying to accomplish? What is its outreach ministry? *Praying* is something that should permeate group life.

Your small-group agenda

As far as the actual agenda for the group meeting is concerned, there are four main components. These agenda items are sharing, Bible study, prayer, and mission. Every type of group follows this same agenda. *Sharing* includes developing friendships, loving, and deciding. *Bible study* includes learning. *Mission* is outreach to others, which is "doing." *Prayer* is seeking God's power in all aspects of group life. Of course, there is some overlap between these components. Different groups will spend different amounts of time on each item. For example, a group whose concentration is on sharing would spend less time in Bible study, mission, and prayer. An outreach Bible study group might spend less time on sharing and prayer.

Following is a sample agenda for two different types of 90-minute group meetings:

Fellowship Group	Outreach Bible Study Group
sharing—50 minutes	sharing—20 minutes
Bible study—25 minutes	Bible study—55 minutes
prayer time—15 minutes	prayer time—15 minutes

Of course, every group must be flexible enough to meet the emergent needs of the group and to follow the leading of the Holy Spirit. This structure is only a beginning point; there is no single right way to organize and conduct a group meeting. Still, the group will follow a basic outline, though the sequence and terminology may vary somewhat from group to group. This basic outline will include these four vital ingredients: sharing questions, Bible study, mission, and prayer. Let's look at each of these in turn.

Sharing questions

In order for the group to be successful, it is important that each member become involved in the discussion and be willing to share openly. To set the stage for each meeting, the group needs to begin with a time of sharing. This sharing time gets everyone relaxed and talking about their week and their personal life in a nonthreatening environment. It helps the members of the group to be aware of each other's needs, and it gets the quiet group members involved right away in the group process, so that they will continue to talk during the study time.

The group leader begins with prayer, then says, "Let's talk about our week. What has happened in your life since our last meeting?" After the members have had time to talk about their week, the group leader asks a question that helps the group members become better acquainted with one another. The purpose is to establish closer relationships. For example, the group leader might ask, "Jesus once told His disciples that they needed to take a break and rest from their work. What do you like to do for rest and relaxation?"

Regarding sharing questions, a key point to remember is that they need to be nonthreatening, allowing the members to share their personal stories. Sharing questions should require no special knowledge of the Bible or any other topic. Sharing time should be nonjudgmental, simple, laid-back, and fun!

Sharing time has several benefits. It gets everyone involved and gives the group members an opportunity to become acquainted, deepen relationships, and make new friends. It provides an opportunity for the members to become aware of and appreciate the uniqueness of one another.

There are basically five types of sharing questions that a group may participate in during the lifetime of the group. These are:

1. *Past-tense sharing questions.* These are questions that allow group members to share about their personal history. The questions assist in understanding fellow members' life experiences and backgrounds. Past-tense questions are especially helpful in the beginning stages of a group. Examples are: "Did you attend church as a child? Which denomination?" "What was your favorite game as a child?" "What was the funniest thing that ever happened at the dinner table in your childhood?" "How was your home heated when you were growing up?"

2. *Present-tense sharing questions.* These are questions that assist the members in talking about what is currently happening in their lives. Examples: "What is your favorite current hobby?" "What is one thing that someone did for you this week that you appreciated?" "Where is your favorite place?"

3. *Future-tense sharing questions.* These questions give the members an opportunity to talk about their hopes and dreams for the future. Examples: "Where would you like to go on your next vacation?" "How would you like to be remembered at the end of your life?"

4. *Affirmation sharing questions.* These questions give the members an opportunity to share positive things about one another. Examples: "How has the group been the most helpful to you?" "What quality do you like best in each person in the group?"

5. *Accountability sharing questions.* This type of question is used *only* if the members have agreed to hold each other mutually accountable for Christian living. This can be a very risky type of question, so use this category with caution. Examples: "How has your prayer and Bible study gone this past week?" "Have you taken quality time each day with your children this past week?"

Here are some important guidelines that leaders need to follow in regard to sharing questions:

1. After asking the question, ask for a volunteer to begin responding. Never go around the circle for responses and put someone on the spot. The leader may need to model the question by responding first.

2. Allow people to choose not to respond to questions if they wish. Say something like "Who would like to be next?" or "It's OK not to share, if that's your choice" or "If you feel you want to pass tonight, that's OK."

3. Choose questions that are not threatening.

4. Do not ask for opinions on controversial topics, such as abortion, capital punishment, etc.

5. Do not ask questions that cause people to be negative about themselves or life. The goal is to create a positive experience, giving the members opportunity to know one another better and to minister to one another.

Bible study

In Christian groups the learning/discussing time should be based on the Bible. Depending on the type of group, other materials may be used, but God's Word needs to be the foundation. A grief recovery group, for example, may use a contemporary book as its main focus, but the Bible should be a key resource.

There are various types of Bible study that can be used in a small group. Some of these are, for example: (a) relational, (b) topical, and (c) devotional Bible study, etc. However, for those who are beginning small-group involvement, I suggest starting with inductive Bible study. Later one can choose other formats of Bible study.

Inductive Bible study is discussion-based study. The leader *facilitates* the discussion, but does not do all the talking. The leader guides the group in discovering the truths to be learned. This style is the opposite of the seminar approach, in which the teacher shares information and answers questions, allowing discussion only when it is needed or as there is time. However, in a small group the leader does sometimes teach, and he or she must always give leadership to the discussion so that it does not become merely a gabfest of personal ideas or a pooling of thoughts with no scriptural basis. The leader must study and prepare in order to guide the discussion gently without dominating the process.

An inductive Bible study has three parts. First there is *observation*. What does the text say? What is the context and background of the passage? At this point the group members simply list the facts and gain as much understanding of the passage as possible. Second, there is *interpretation*. What does the text mean? This involves reviewing the historical and textual context and asking what the text meant when it was originally written. Third is *application*. What parallels can we find between the original context and the contemporary situation? How does the text apply to us today? In this step members ask, "So what? What difference does this text make to me today?"

The ultimate goal of small-group Bible study is application. One must always remember that Scripture is not just for learning; it is for living. If someone in your group is in the middle of a divorce, they will be more concerned about the personal help Jesus can provide right now through the power of the Holy Spirit than they will be with understanding Jesus' genealogy.

One question that often arises as small groups begin to study the Bible is: What study materials should be used? Experience has shown that it is best for a beginning group to use published materials and study guides, as opposed to leader-prepared material. Printed guides have usually been written by someone who has experience in small-group life, and the study guides are designed to help the group follow a pattern to ensure a more positive experience.

Mission

Every group must have a well-defined purpose and outreach strategy that group members understand and own. It is critical that members understand the reason for their existence as a group and feel a sense of ownership of group life. Experience has shown that without an outreach strategy, the focus of the group will turn inward, the members' excitement and sense of fulfillment will decline, and group life will stagnate and deteriorate.

I saw this happen in a church I was visiting. I met with the small-group leaders for a training and question-and-answer session. Alice asked me why I thought her small group had stagnated and died. Her group had begun with six members excited about studying, praying, and experiencing fellowship together. Together they established goals, but after eight months interest had waned, and the group had ceased to exist. After a brief discussion I discovered that two months after it began meeting, Alice's group changed its focus. The members decided to let no new individuals into the group, they dropped all outreach, (because everyone was too busy), and they began focusing on their own needs rather than the needs of others. Alice told me that the group members were afraid new people would destroy their close-knit community. The group violated the divine principle that reaching out to others gives life to all who are part of the process.

A thriving group will reach out to non-Christians, to Christians who do not have a growing relationship with Jesus Christ, and to Christians of all denominations who are searching for a deeper understanding of Scripture.

Certain types of groups are outreach groups automatically by their design and purpose. Other groups, such as a Christian prayer group, or a group of church members studying a book about last-day events, such as *The Great Controversy,* may need to formulate an outreach strategy or project in order to keep the group healthy and to fulfill the scriptural mandate.

Prayer

Prayer is the lifeblood of the group. Prayer bonds group members together, strengthens members for daily life, and undergirds the working of the Holy Spirit in the group. Prayer strengthens group relationships, assists members in developing a devotional life, enables members to minister to one another, and builds faith as members see God meeting the daily needs of those in the group.

It is safe to assume that some in the group have never before prayed privately and that some have never prayed publicly. Others are scared to pray out loud and might never join a group if they think they might be put on the spot to do so. A good rule to follow is to let the group members know that they will never be asked to pray out loud. Prayer time must always be voluntary.

Involving group members in prayer

There are, however, several ideas that a group leader can use to involve the entire group in prayer.

1. Provide written prayers for all the members to read out loud together at the end of the prayer time. Use the Lord's Prayer, the twenty-third psalm, or a written prayer.

2. Give every member a card on which a passage of Scripture has been written and invite anyone who wants to read the card out loud during the prayer time to do so.

3. Distribute paper and pencils and ask the members to write out a sentence prayer and read it during the prayer time.

4. During prayer time, pray a short, one-sentence prayer and ask the members to fill in the blanks with only one or two words. For example, the leader could pray, "Lord, help me to . . ." or "Lord, thank You for . . ."

5. Suggest that the group members pray by category, offering sentence prayers of praise to God, sentence prayers asking God to meet the needs of those outside the group, or sentence prayers asking God to meet the needs of those within the group.

6. Have a period of silent prayer.

7. One small group I visited wrote a Bible text on a whiteboard that the group members could read together at the end of the prayer time.

Usually at the beginning of the group meeting, the leader or a group member will say a prayer. During the main meeting, either at the end or during the sharing time, the members will have their time of prayer together. Often this is conversational prayer. The prayers are short—one or two sentences. A person can pray more than once. The group does not go around the circle; instead, the prayers are spontaneous and voluntary. Some call these "popcorn prayers."

The group should keep a prayer journal of requests and God's answers. It can also be helpful to form prayer partners once the group members have bonded with one another and are comfortable with the idea.

Types of groups

In the preceding pages we have focused upon a typical home Bible study group that follows an agenda that arises from Acts 2:41-47. This agenda has four parts: (1) sharing, (2) Bible study, (3) prayer, and (4) mission. The group meets for approximately 90 minutes once a week. New group members are invited weekly, with the goal in mind of leading the group members into accepting Jesus as Lord and Savior of their lives through a study of various topics of the Bible.

STEP ONE: Draw a horizontal line.

STEP TWO: Draw a cross at the center of the line.

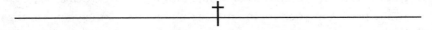

STEP THREE: Draw 10 perpendicular lines on either side of the cross.

STEP FOUR: Number the lines from -10 to -1 on the left side, and +1 to +10 on the right.

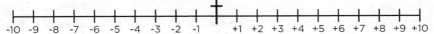

-10 -9 -8 -7 -6 -5 -4 -3 -2 -1   +1 +2 +3 +4 +5 +6 +7 +8 +9 +10

EXPLANATION	*The cross represents the point at which a person accepts Jesus Christ as Lord and Savior of his or her life.*
The lines numbered +1 to +10 on the right side of the cross indicate the journey a new Christian takes following his or her acceptance of Jesus.	
Numbers +1 to +3	represent the new Christian developing a devotional life (prayer, Bible study, and sharing their faith).
Numbers +4 to +7	represent the discovering of one's spiritual gifts and becoming equipped and involved in ministry.
Numbers +8 to +10	represent a fully devoted disciple of Jesus involved in ministry, leadership, and discipling others.
The lines numbered -1 to -10 represent how far a person is from accepting Jesus.	
Numbers -1 to -3	represent an individual who is a spiritual seeker, willing to discuss spiritual topics, and be involved in a Bible study group.
Numbers -4 to -6	represent someone who has some interest in spiritual themes, but who will not participate in a Bible study group.
Numbers -7 and -8	represent those who may seek spiritual help if they have a crisis or personal need such as a funeral or wedding. Other than that, spirituality is at the bottom of their list.
Numbers - 9 and -10	represent those who have absolutely no interest at any time in spiritual issues.

The goal should be to have every church member be part of a small group and have an Acts 2:41-47 experience. In addition, we want our friends, neighbors, family, work associates, and others in our community to attend a Bible study group with us. However, not every unchurched person will want to be a member of a Bible study group. So if I want to invite my friends who have little or no desire to study the Bible to become involved in a small-group experience, what should I do?

I like to answer this question using a four-step illustration that I call the Evangelism Scale. (It's based on and adapted from the Engle Scale.)

All the people in your community are represented somewhere on this scale. The ones who would sit in a Bible study group are those to the right of the cross (+1 to +10) who are already Christians. Those who do not profess to be active Christians—those to the left of the cross—will not usually attend a small-group Bible study, except those in the −1 to −3 category. What do we do about the others?

As Christians we are fully committed to taking the gospel to every person. As did Jesus, we are to "seek and save the lost." This means everyone. Jesus died for all. So we cannot have the attitude that if we invite someone to our Bible study group, cell group, or house church and that person will not come, we have fulfilled our duty and we now can shake the dust from our feet.

The apostle Paul said, "For though I am free from all men, I have made myself a servant to all, that I might win the more" (1 Cor. 9:19). He goes on to say he became as a Jew, as a man under the law, and as one who is weak, that he "might by all means save some" (verse 22).

Jesus was accused of hanging out with tax collectors and sinners (see Luke 15:1, 2). Ellen White, reflecting on Jesus' lifestyle, wrote: "Christ's method alone will give true success in reaching the people. The Saviour mingled with men as one who desired their good. He showed His sympathy for them, ministered to their needs, and won their confidence. Then He bade them, 'Follow Me.'" [5]

In other words, Jesus went where the people were. We must do the same in terms of small groups! Yes, just as Jesus wants everyone to accept Him as Lord and Savior, so we want everyone eventually to have an Acts 2:41-47 experience—a wholistic small-group experience, as some would call it. But in order to get people to this point in their lives, we must meet them where they are in their life experience. As society has become more secular and postmodern, interest in religion and objective truth about God has declined.[6] Thus one must do something to attract the attention of friends and neighbors who have little interest in a religious discussion. This means we will have what I call *first-step small groups*.

Introduction to first-step small groups

As I think about this "stepped approach," which is a different concept than was common among most small groups of 15 years ago, I am reminded of the following:

The house church that met in the home of Aquila and Priscilla (see 1 Cor. 16:19) was a far cry from our prevailing twenty-first-century concept that every church congregation must have a building and a full-time, paid pastor to guide the church. The size of a home church was limited by the number of participants that could squeeze into a house. The services were likely very interactive because of the small number of attendees.

Likewise, the Waldensian small groups, meeting in a cave or secretly around a campfire in the Piedmont of Italy, followed a very different model than the Wesleyan approach in eighteenth-century Britain. John Wesley's "societies" divided into "classes," which met weekly with an assigned leader. Bible study, commitment to a Christian lifestyle, prayer, and collecting an offering were integral parts of the Wesleyan small-group experience.

The small-group meeting in a park or a coffeehouse during the seventies in America was geared to meet the needs of flower children, Jesus people, and those seeking "freedom" through a "psychedelic" lifestyle of drugs, free love, and rebellion against authority. In theory, this model is similar to—but a far cry from—today's Starbucks Bible study group, reading Scripture from iPhones, e-readers, Blackberries, PDAs, and laptops.

Today we see many successful and/or expanding models of small groups or cell churches. In my lifetime I can recall a number of small-group models that have arrived on the church scene—Body Life, Serendipity, Touch Ministries, Meta-Church, Group of Twelve (G12), Simple Church, Free Market Cells, and a Seeker Model. This is by no means a complete list. I have personally visited or experienced AYA groups, Park Evangelism Small Groups, Homes of Hope, Cell Church, Home Bible Fellowships, and Growth Groups, to name a few.

A look at each of these models reveals differences in organization, meeting format, and structure. However, you will find common ingredients in almost every model. These reflect the principles of Acts 2—building relationships, supporting/meeting needs of group members, accountability, application of Scripture to everyday life, praying together, reaching out to those who are spiritual inquirers, leading people to Jesus/making disciples, and mobilizing the entire church for service.

The *big* difference, as you may have noticed, is that culture, circumstances, and time (the year and century) dictate what the group "looks like" in terms of organization and structure. The church must always be culturally relevant—moving with the times—which means that there cannot be a single "correct" model for small groups. One caution, however: do not be so culturally relevant that you forget the mission of the church—to bring people to Jesus, who came "to seek and to save" the lost (Luke 19:10).

Understanding first-step small groups

First-step small groups begin with only one of the small-group characteristics—friendship. The group accepts individuals just as they are, with no conditions attached. Next we add another characteristic: we minister to their needs. We are caring, sympathetic, helpful, and trusting. Next, after some time and with God's leading, a "pathway" is opened by which we are able to talk with them about spiritual things. Next, we are able to explore with them the basics of the gospel. And finally, we are able to guide them into the Acts 2:41-47 small-group experience.

In order to give every person in our community an opportunity to have such a small-group experience, and in order for us to become acquainted with them, there are a variety of types of small groups. I believe that every church should always have Bible study groups in place that are patterned after the Acts 2:41-47 model and that it should then add some of the other types of groups as needed or as there is an interest.

Types of small groups

There are many types of small groups. Each group follows the format discussed earlier in this chapter—sharing, Bible study, prayer, and mission. The difference is in the emphasis and the amount of time spent on each item. Some of the most common types of groups are:

1. *A fellowship group* is designed for social interaction. The group time may not follow the four-step outline given above very closely. Members may get excited about relationships and group activities, such as potlucks, shopping, picnics, hikes, trips to the zoo, etc. This type of group is especially helpful for new members, the lonely, singles, and those who love people and having a good time. A fellowship group must intentionally develop an outreach project for the group to do together, or outreach will be overlooked. The weakness of fellowship groups is that they may get so caught up in social activities that Bible study and prayer are overlooked.

2. *A Bible study group* is for those who like to study the Bible and other books together with other Christians in order to grow in their knowledge of a particular topic. This group may study a book of the Bible, or a topic such as last-day events, angels, etc. The weakness with this group is that it can develop an attitude that "we alone have the truth." This type of group, too, needs an outreach project in order to maintain balance.

3. *Outreach groups* are designed to reach out to non-Christians, the unchurched, or nonattending church members. There are a variety of approaches. *One* example is a study group. The study may focus on various books of the Bible or on such topics as angels, the life of Jesus, etc. The Homes of Hope program that was developed in the Oregon Conference of Seventh-day Adventists, which I mentioned in the introduction of this book, is an example of an outreach group.

A *second* type of outreach group is sometimes called a pathway or a redemptive friendship group. This type is called a "pathway" group because it meets personal needs and directs people down the path toward Jesus. Some individuals suggest using a name for the group that reflects the group's purpose of touching the needs of people's lives.[7] The group members provide a "healing touch" rooted in the grace and compassion of Christ. These groups focus not on books of the Bible, but on people's needs. An example is MOMS, mothers of preschool children. Another may be a men's or women's breakfast group in which the focus is on friendships and the fact that Jesus can make a difference in the issues of daily life.

A *third* type of outreach group is designed to meet the needs of those who were once Christians or who currently are sporadic church attendees.

The purpose of this type of group is to reacquaint these people with Jesus. A *fourth* type is a seeker group. This group is designed with secular people in mind. The group may be for atheists or for those who are unfamiliar with religious themes and concepts. Touch groups also minister to those in categories three and four.

The weakness of outreach groups is that they may focus on numerical growth rather than the spiritual growth of the members.

4. Task/ministry groups are outreach and nurture groups in which the members do not spend the majority of their time sitting in a circle. In fact, many task groups meet only once a month to spend an hour or more in the circle; I suggest the time be divided into sharing, a brief Bible study, ministry planning, and prayer. The other weeks, meet for a short time of sharing, reflecting on a scriptural promise; have prayer; and then turn to the chosen task. One example is a literature task group that hands out literature door-to-door, manages literature news boxes and public display racks, etc. Other examples may be groups made up of Pathfinder leaders, choir members, or Sabbath school division leaders and assistants. These individuals meet weekly or bimonthly to discuss their ministry, support one another, have a brief study together, pray, and do ministry together.

Task groups need to look for outreach opportunities. For the Pathfinders, it may be getting unchurched youth and their parents involved in church activities. For the children's Sabbath school, it may be visiting nonattending parents whose children attend Sabbath school.

The theme of a task/ministry group is that God has given everyone a spiritual gift and it needs to be used in ministry. The weakness of this type of group is that the task may become more important than relationships, Bible study, or prayer.

5. Support groups are designed for individuals with special needs. These needs are usually short-term, with the members going on to join another type of group. Examples of support groups are groups focused on divorce, grief recovery, addictions (alcohol, drugs, tobacco, eating disorders, etc.), or other similar needs. *The groups are for support, not therapy. If an individual needs therapy, it should be received from a professional Christian counselor.* The group members are aware of their mutual struggles, but this is not the focus of the group. The group focuses on friendship, studying the Bible as a source of assistance, and praying for each other. Often a relevant book or other material is used as a supplement to the Bible.

I have visited support groups that included individuals with a variety of needs, such as bulimia, alcohol addiction, divorce recovery, and tobacco addiction. The group members shared how their week had gone, then shared a Bible study centering on how God was the solution to their needs. The group members ended their meeting by joining hands and standing in a circle, praying for one another.

The weakness of support groups is that the members may tend to focus upon their individual needs rather than upon the power of the Holy Spirit and being re-created in Jesus.

6. *Prayer groups* spend the majority of their time in prayer, although these groups also include Bible study and sharing. The members usually have prayer partners, prayer chains, or networks, and are willing to pray as needed for situations and circumstances that are brought to their attention. The weakness of prayer groups is the danger of viewing others as less spiritual if they do not belong to a prayer group or if they do not pray as much as group members do.

7. *Wholistic Bible study groups* are made up of members who want to have a balance in the use of their group time, focusing on the four ingredients of sharing: Bible study, outreach, ministry, and prayer. Usually the group studies a book of the Bible or a biblical topic. The group members have an open-group policy and invite new people to join the group on a weekly basis. During their prayer time, the members pray for new people to come each week.

This type of group is a popular one, because it incorporates all aspects of a small group in a manner that most easily meets the needs of most people. In addition, it meets the biblical criteria of small-group life. The weakness of this type of group is that members may lose their balance and focus on one aspect of the group-meeting format. In addition, they may forget to invite new people and focus on process rather than outreach. Also, a constant influx of people may prevent the group from developing a sense of cohesiveness.

8. *A house church* is technically not a small group but sometimes functions like one. It meets in a home rather than a church building. All aspects of church life are usually present in the home setting. On Sabbath morning there is a Sabbath school and worship service. During the week there is a small-group meeting. Board meetings or planning sessions are held in the home setting.

In some countries that prohibit public Christian meetings, this is how church life is lived out. It is also an outreach strategy in some countries. When I was in Brazil conducting small-group training, I discovered some of the members developing plans to plant new churches using this strategy. In North America branch Sabbath schools were based on the same premise. It is time, I believe, that we begin using small groups as a church-planting strategy.

The weakness of the house church is that it can become isolated from the larger community of the church, forgetting the need to function within denominational guidelines and failing to cooperate with the corporate church. On occasion, independent churches have taken a radical direction that has led them into unsound doctrine.

9. *A cell church* is a church in which all the members belong to a small group. All of church life occurs in the cell. There are usually very few programs, and nothing is allowed to compete with the cell, including board meetings. Even the weekly worship service is secondary to cell life. Numerous churches outside North America follow this model, and several in North America strive to perfect this model. Many individuals and organizations are working hard on this concept that some say is the church of the future.

The weakness of the cell church is that it too can become isolated from the larger community of the church and not see the value in large group meetings (worship service, etc.).

10. *Sabbath school action units* are based upon the premise that the Adventist Church already has a built-in small-group philosophy and structure—the Sabbath school—that is not being used to its full capacity. The premise is that the purpose of the Sabbath school is fellowship, ministry training, Bible study, outreach (local and worldwide), and prayer support— and that since these are the biblical ingredients for a small-group format, they should be incorporated into the Sabbath school every Sabbath morning in each class. The classes are given a minimum of one hour in which to follow the small-group format of sharing, study, prayer, and working on an outreach project. Sometimes the class project may be a small home group during the week. The home group and Sabbath school class can then work together as a unit for more success.

The weakness of the Sabbath school action unit is that, in some cases, the location of the class and the time available are not conducive to healthy group life. Often the members sit in pews together with other classes in the sanctuary. Because of inadequate time and a less-than-ideal location, the group interaction is not as bonding as it could be. This leads to discouragement and lack of participation by the members and a negative attitude toward small groups in general.

11. A mission group develops a plan to take the gospel into a particular community, people group, or unreached population segment. The group mission plan includes all four of the key elements of Acts 2:42-47 (doctrine, fellowship, breaking of bread, and prayer). One example would be a small group of Spanish-speaking members in an Anglo congregation who come together to plant a new church in a Hispanic community. Another example would be a group that starts a ministry on a nearby state university campus.

In summary, be flexible. Remember the core values of small groups and the previously stated biblical principles. They are timeless. How a culture, a generation, or a local church carries them out is optional. However, we must not make optional methods, models, and applications an excuse to ignore God's plan of meeting "house to house" and in the "temple."

Categories or types of groups

Several have taken the preceding types of small groups and have divided them under main categories for easier identification. For example, the terms "Mary groups" and "Martha groups" are used, based upon the Bible story of Mary sitting at the feet of Jesus while Martha fixed the meal. Those who sit in the weekly circle groups for daily nurture belong to "Mary groups." Those who prefer action rather than weekly circle groups belong to "Martha groups."

Mary Groups	Martha Groups
fellowship groups	some outreach groups
Bible study groups	house church
outreach groups	Sabbath school action units
prayer groups	mission group
support groups	
covenant groups	

Here is another three-way division of groups:

Task Groups	Fellowship Groups	Bible Study
outreach	fellowship	Bible study
support	covenant	Sabbath school action unit
Sabbath school action unit	prayer	
house church		
mission group		

Others have divided small groups into "community groups" (those that bridge to the community), "disciple-making groups" (those that assist Christians), and "serving groups" (those that provide ministry opportunities to utilize spiritual gifts).

There may be some overlap in these categories. One must also keep in mind that the various types of groups all follow the same agenda of sharing, Bible study, prayer, and mission. However, the amount of time a group spends in any specific area may vary depending upon the type of group and its mission. The following diagrams illustrate this idea:

Study and Support Groups

Outreach-focused Groups   Ministry or Task Groups   Christian Fellowship Groups

A healthy small group

A healthy small group will be one that is open to everyone no matter what his or her need may be. It is true that at times the special needs of a person may dictate that another type of group would better meet his or her need, but the group leader will assist that person in joining the group that is best for the individual. One must also keep in mind the importance of the affinity factor—that is, that people with similar needs draw strength and support from seeking God together. A healthy group would look something like this:

The next chapter will provide job descriptions and a further explanation of these leadership and participant roles.

A Healthy Small Group

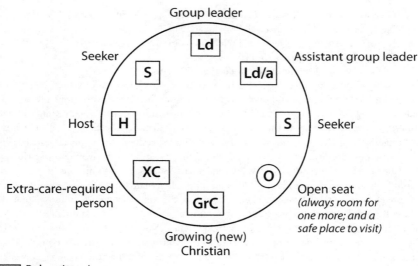

Kathy's two sons had left home. One was married; the other was in college. As she adjusted to her new lifestyle, Kathy thought that a small group studying various biblical topics with other empty-nesters would be an excellent outreach opportunity for her at this time. She looked around and discovered that neighbors, work associates, friends from church, and other general acquaintances were in the same stage of life in which she found herself. She invited them to join a small group with others like themselves.

The affinity factor was not their religious beliefs or backgrounds, but their stage in life. This provided an opportunity for a group of women to support one another, pray together, study the Bible together, and make new friends in a nonthreatening environment.

This type of group is sometimes called a "pathway group" or a "bridging group." Such a group allows members to form relationships that later provide opportunities to invite someone to study major teachings of the Bible or attend other church functions and, eventually, evangelistic reaping meetings. This is true friendship evangelism at its finest!

----

[1] Gregory Lawson, in *Christian Educational Journal* 13, no. 3 (Spring 1993): 67.

[2] Neal McBride, *How to Lead Small Groups,* p. 24.

[3] Roberta Hestenes, class lectures, Fuller Theological Seminary, 1986.

[4] Ellen G. White, *Evangelism,* p. 115.

[5] Ellen G. White, *The Ministry of Healing,* p. 143.

[6] Barna Group, one of the major sources of trends and statistics regarding religion and spirituality in America, has synthesized its findings from interviews with thousands of individuals during 2009. The report includes the following major themes: "Theme 1: Increasingly, Americans are more interested in faith and spirituality than in Christianity. Faith remains a hot topic in America these days. . . . Politicians, athletes, cultural philosophers, teachers, entertainers, musicians—nearly everyone has something to say about faith, religion, spirituality, mortality, and belief these days. But as the fundamental values and assumptions of our nation continue to shift, so do our ideas of faith and spirituality. Many of our basic assumptions are no longer firm or predictable. . . . Theme 2: Faith in the American context is now individual and customized. Americans are comfortable with an altered spiritual experience as long as they can participate in the shaping of that experience. Now that we are comfortable with the idea of being spiritual as opposed to devoutly Christian, . . . Americans typically draw from a broad treasury of moral, spiritual, and ethical sources of thought to concoct a uniquely personal brand of faith. Feeling freed from the boundaries established by the Christian faith, and immersed in a postmodern society which revels in participation, personal expression, satisfying relationships, and authentic experiences, we become our own unchallenged spiritual authorities, defining truth and reality as we see fit. . . . In some ways, we are creating the ultimate ecumenical movement, where nothing is deemed right or wrong, and all ideas, beliefs, and practices are assigned equal validity. . . . Only one third (34 percent) [of American adults] believe in absolute moral truth. . . . Theme 3: Biblical literacy is neither a current reality nor a goal in the U.S. Barna's findings related to Bible knowledge and application indicate that little progress, if any, is being made toward assisting people to become more biblically literate." (Source: www.barna.org/barna-update/article/12-faithspirituality/325-barna-studies-the-research-offers-a-year-in-review-perspective.)

[7]Monte Sahlin, director of research and special projects for the Ohio Conference of Seventh-day Adventists, shared this suggestion, along with several other helpful insights for this section.

Chapter 6

SMALL GROUPS 201—
UNDERSTANDING YOUR GROUP

I was sitting in a Sabbath school class in Vancouver, Washington. The class teacher welcomed every member and visitor in a manner that would put the pacing lion at the Portland Zoo at ease. He then said, "We have several class styles in our church. In my class I do most of the talking. I like doing research and sharing the ideas and information I find. I invite you to participate, but I have a certain amount of information that I want to share. If any of you prefer more discussion and interaction, there is a class that meets in the classroom across the hall. The members sit in a circle and discuss their viewpoints on Scripture. If you prefer that type of learning experience, it won't offend me if you join the small-group Bible study."

This teacher unintentionally summarized two basic approaches to sharing biblical knowledge—(1) the teacher-centered approach (the didactic method), and (2) the student-centered approach (the inductive method).

The didactic method is more instructional. The teacher tells the students the information. The teacher designs the class outline and decides what to emphasize. The didactic approach includes an emphasis on information. Learning is primarily through participation and interaction from teacher to student or student to teacher—rarely student to student. The following diagram illustrates this didactic approach.

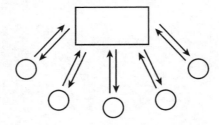

The inductive method, or student-centered approach, is discovery learning. The teacher facilitates learning as a group leader rather than as an authority who imparts knowledge. The group leader outlines and prepares information to share, but prefers to help the students discover answers to questions for themselves rather than just tell them the answers. This approach focuses on the student and provides a process for them to grow through discovering knowledge rather than through just receiving the teacher's knowledge.

The inductive method involves an emphasis on the process of individual discovery. It includes the student deciding what is important to learn; teaching through participation; and interaction from leader to student, student to leader, and student to student.

The following diagram illustrates the inductive approach:

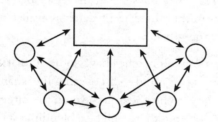

How do these two methods work in a teaching/learning environment? In the didactic approach, the teacher seeks to:

- *understand the students' Bible knowledge.* That is, the teacher learns what the students already understand about a given subject.
- *impart knowledge.* Once the teacher has determined the students' level of understanding on a topic, he or she determines what information to teach.
- *inspire desire.* Biblical facts and principles are to be not only learned but lived. The goal of the teacher is to motivate the students to apply what they have learned to their lives.
- *generate action.* The teacher makes specific suggestions on how the students can respond to God's Word. The goal is for the students to make life-changing decisions.

In the inductive approach, the teacher:

- *begins with a basic question.* After selecting a passage of Scripture and identifying the topic for discussion, the teacher presents questions to stimulate discussion. The students will reveal their understanding through their input in the discussion.
- *suggests resources for understanding.* As the discussion and interchange of ideas takes place, the teacher suggests books, Web sites, other passages of Scripture, etc., that will assist the students in discovering the desired answer. The teacher guides the students to sources of information instead of stating the facts.
- *assists the students in evaluation.* Once facts are discovered, the students and teacher discuss together how these facts affect their lives. Together they evaluate the implications of their conclusions.
- *mentors the students.* Once the students have decided to take a specific action or direction in their lives, the teacher is available for accountability and assistance in the journey.

As you can see, both approaches have some similarities, and both have the same target or result in mind—discovering life-changing biblical truth. It is the approach—how to hit the bull's-eye on the target—that is different. In some small-group settings there will be a blending of the two approaches. However, most small groups will use the inductive (discovery) approach.

In small groups that use the inductive approach the teacher is called a group leader and the student is called a group member.

The following diagrams further illustrate three commonly used methods of interaction and learning.

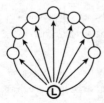
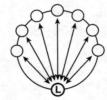

Preaching, Lecturing   Teaching, Seminars   Small Group

I was leading a small-group weekly Bible study on the Gospel of John. During our study on John 3 we read verse 5, in which Jesus states one must be "born of water and the Spirit" to enter the kingdom of God. I asked: "What does it mean to be born of water and the Spirit?"

Steve responded, "It means that we are to be baptized, and I think it is by being dipped under the water."

Jana added, "I was sprinkled as a baby and not put under the water. Does it make a difference?"

As the discussion continued, I said to the group members, "There seems to be quite an interest on the topic of baptism. This week let's each find all the Bible texts and material on the topic that we can and bring the information with you next week for a discussion. Does that sound OK to everyone?" The group members all agreed.

Now, I could have explained baptism to the group members and directed them to the key texts on the subject. Instead, I waited to bring my texts to the next week's discussion in order to allow the group members to research and study on their own. This approach takes longer, but a person usually remembers longer and better what they have discovered than what the leader tells them.

When the discovery method of learning is followed in a small group, it differs somewhat from a classroom style of teaching. Some of the differences are:

1. The small-group meeting is normally held in a home rather than in the church or a public building. I have attended small-group meetings in a funeral home, in offices at lunch hour, and in a restaurant. Any nonthreatening location will work.

2. The seating arrangement is with chairs in a circle, rather than in a row. A living room or kitchen table is an excellent setting. It is key that no one sit outside the circle, or the group dynamic will be lost.

3. Group meetings are usually held one night (or day) per week for an hour and a half in length. It is important to begin and end on time, or some members may stop attending. Members need their sleep, and some may need to get children to bed.

4. Rather than a prepared lecture by a teacher, there is a leader-guided discussion. Nevertheless, preparation is still essential. Some group leaders make the mistake of not studying the material before the meeting. A leader who does not understand the material cannot guide the discussion. At times it is necessary for the leader to assume the role of teacher for a short period

of time. To say that teaching is never an aspect of a small group is not reality. But the leader is a facilitator, not a lecturer.

5. The focus of the study time is on developing interpersonal relationships and the application of biblical knowledge to everyday life. Understanding Scripture and knowing doctrine is important, but life application is crucial in a small-group setting. Remember, Scripture is not only for learning; it is also for living.

6. It is important to call for decision responses throughout the group time together, but not to the point that members feel pressured or some stop attending. The key is to keep group members attending in order to give the Holy Spirit opportunity to convict hearts.

7. The maximum number of participants in many small groups is approximately 12. Sometimes more than 12 can participate, depending on the type of house meeting. In contrast, a lecture-style class approach can accommodate a larger number.

8. In a small group it is very important to be sensitive to the spiritual growth of the members and not share too much information too fast. The apostle Paul told the Corinthian believers, "And I, brethren, could not speak to you as to spiritual people but as to carnal, as to babes in Christ. I fed you with milk and not with solid food; for until now you were not able to receive it" (1 Cor. 3:1, 2). Ellen White, commenting upon the same topic, wrote: "You need not feel that all the truth is to be spoken to unbelievers on any and every occasion. You should plan carefully what to say and what to leave unsaid. This is not practicing deception; it is to work as Paul worked."*

Location and leadership

Location. Choosing the location of your group is critical to its success. An uncomfortably cold or warm room, noisy children, or pets can distract group members. In selecting a location, choose wisely. Careful planning should provide:

- a comfortable atmosphere in the living room or around the kitchen table.
- good lighting. This is necessary for study and developing a warm atmosphere.

- seating in a circle, so that everyone can see one another as they talk.
- a location that will provide the fewest distractions and interruptions. Children, pets, telephones, television, radios, etc., can disrupt your study group.
- child care if necessary in order for some group members to attend. If a home has the space, a volunteer may be found to take care of the children.

Leadership. A separate chapter will deal with leadership in small groups, so a brief job description for the group leader will suffice for this section. A small-group leader is the person appointed and recognized to serve the group by facilitating and enabling the group to achieve its purposes and goals. The *leader* does this by:

- attending a leadership training workshop after participating in a small group as an assistant leader or member.
- facilitating the weekly group meeting.
- overseeing all details of group life within and outside of the weekly meeting.
- modeling and encouraging participation, sharing, acceptance, and understanding among the members.
- guiding the group in developing and carrying out a "group agreement" (covenant) and goals.
- checking on members who are absent from the meeting in order to encourage, meet needs, and to be aware of difficulties. (Assistant leader and host can assist.)
- talking and praying weekly about the group with the assistant leader and with the host.
- seeking assistance as needed to ensure positive group life.
- attending regularly scheduled leaders' meetings.

The *assistant leader* should:

- support, encourage, and pray for the leader.
- facilitate the group meeting when the leader is absent.
- assist in recruitment of new members and the follow-up of absent members.

- assist with such details as child care or program arrangements, preparing and submitting required reports, and other details as needed.
- attend monthly leaders' meetings.
- be an apprentice in training to lead a group of their own in the future.

The *host* should:

- provide a comfortable home or other location for the meeting.
- arrange seating in the meeting room; adjust temperature, oversee refreshments (if applicable), and make sure extra Bibles, paper, study guides, pencils, etc., are available.
- answer the door and welcome the members as they arrive.
- make sure the members' needs are met—directing them to the location of the bathroom, telephone, etc.
- take care of distractions that may occur during the group meeting, such as the doorbell, telephone, children, pets, etc.
- oversee the preparation/availability of food/treats and a special drink if they are part of your group.

These three leadership positions are important to the success of a small group. However, spiritual preparation is the first and most important step. Through the power of the Holy Spirit, the least-experienced individual can be dramatically effective. The spiritual success of the group is dependent, not upon the talents or abilities of the leaders, but upon the willingness of the group members to yield themselves to the will and power of God.

The group agreement (covenant)

It is essential that the group come to an understanding concerning its expectations for the meeting and the relationships between members. A group agreement will solve many difficulties and prevent many problems before they start. An agreement, or covenant, defines group members' expectations, provides a mechanism for accountability to one another, enhances commitment to the group, provides a basis by which to evaluate the group's success, and establishes the purpose of the group.

At the first group meeting, the leader should help members become acquainted with each other, share basic information, and tell the members that the next week they will discuss in detail the issues and agenda of their small-group time together. The topics to cover at this second meeting are:

- The group is a safe place to be. Members are accepted just as they are.
- No one will ever be put on the spot or intentionally embarrassed. Talking, praying, or reading aloud within the group will be a voluntary choice on the part of each member. The leader will not go around the circle and ask anyone to do anything. (If the group members agree to "going around the circle," it is OK to do so, but I would not do this until the group members have bonded with each other. Otherwise some group members may not return if they feel uncomfortable.)
- The group members will not try to "fix" anyone, but will let the Holy Spirit change and convict people.
- The group goal is to share the experience with others. Eventually the group will multiply and form a new group under the direction of the assistant leader.
- Basic ground rules include the day to meet, the time to begin and end, the need for child care, the length of time (weeks, months) that the group will meet, the importance of calling the leader if a member will miss the meeting (so that the group won't wait for him or her), and other pertinent concerns raised by the leader and members.
- The group should decide on the length of time to spend on the four parts of group life—sharing, study, prayer, and mission.
- The group should discuss the process for inviting new people into the group once the group has been meeting for an extended period of time.

Once the group agreement has been discussed, the members should respect one another and the leader by assisting in carrying out the details of the agreement. Here is a sample form to use in developing a group agreement:

GROUP AGREEMENT

Type of group: _____ Purpose:_____

Meeting location _____

Weekday: _____ Beginning time: _____ Closing time:_____

Our group will meet for _____ months

Our weekly meeting schedule will be: _____

Individual preparation needed (group meeting only or outside of group):

_____

Group leader (name and phone): _____

Assistant leader (name and phone): _____

Host (name and phone): _____

We wish our group to be

☐ open continually to new members

☐ open for _____ weeks

Additional elements we want to be a part of our group:

_____

Ground rules we agree to abide by:

1. We will do our best to be on time for the meetings. If we cannot attend, we will phone the leader or another member to let them know.

2. We will look for ways to assist the leaders and other members in making the group experience as positive as possible.

3. We will share our own personal feelings, but also come willing to listen to others as they share.

4. We will respect the differences in one another and not try to change them. Change is God's responsibility. Our responsibility is love, caring, acceptance, and respect.

5. What group members share in the group will be confidential.

6. Other: _____

_____

Every small group has a distinct personality and set of characteristics that make it unique. Here are some tips about the agreement that are applicable to most groups and that will make life easier for the group:

First, discuss the type of group (fellowship, support, prayer, outreach, etc.) that you are forming. The type of group is determined by its primary focus—the reason for which the group exists.

Second, let the purpose of the group arise out of the type of group. For example, the purpose of a grief recovery group may be to assist members in dealing with the issues of loss. An outreach Bible study may assist members in understanding how God can make a difference in the issues of daily life.

Third, the group should decide when it will meet and the length of the meeting. This will guarantee more participation. Some churches attempt to have all groups meet on the same night and at the same time. This option should be carefully examined to see if it will have a positive or negative effect on attendance. It is essential to begin and end on time. Some individuals have to arise early to go to work. This means that a late-evening meeting usually excludes them.

Fourth, in discussing the schedule and format of the meeting, determine the amount of time that will be spent on sharing, study, prayer, and discussing the group mission. This will assure a balance that all the members can live with and will assist the leader in keeping the group on schedule. Most groups meet for less than two hours per meeting, so the time is limited. In addition, the group needs to talk about how long it will meet before a transition is made and it reorganizes. I am of the opinion that, if possible, everyone in the church should be in some type of group, but that periodically—whenever the current study material is completed, for example—the group should provide a transition time for the members. However, if a group is growing and dividing by constantly adding new members, transitioning becomes an ongoing process. I would also suggest that growing and dividing is the healthiest way for groups to transition.

Fifth, the group should discuss whether or not there will be homework assignments. If time must be spent outside of the group in individual preparation, this may keep some from attending. Openly discuss this issue so that members will not be discouraged.

Once the group agreement (covenant) is discussed and agreed upon, the group members will have ownership of the group, and the leader will have the permission and the responsibility to carry out the details. In addition, the agreement gives the group a tool to use in the future when members discuss how the group is doing in meeting their needs and expectations.

The leaders' meeting

Another absolute essential to a successful small-group ministry is a regular leaders' meeting. Experience indicates that when a group ministry is first beginning, for a few weeks a weekly leaders' meeting is essential. Once the group ministry is established, a meeting once a month is usually sufficient. Do not overextend the group leader's time commitment. If the leaders feel overburdened, they will burn out. Keep open communication with the leaders to make sure their lives are in balance.

The purposes of the meeting are to: (1) cast and build the vision, (2) learn skills, (3) share ideas and problems, pray together, and report. There are various names given to the leadership meetings and to the various segments of the meeting. A common name is VHS meeting, which is an acronym for "vision, huddle, and skill training." The pastor and an assigned coordinator (a church member) should be present. The pastor should do the monthly vision building, so that the group leaders and the pastor continue to work off the same page. The reporting can be done by the lay leader, and the training can be by the pastor, lay leader, a guest, videotape, audiotape, book assignments, and discussion.

The leaders' meeting gives the leaders support, an opportunity to share joys and frustrations, a chance to share solutions to group problems, and a time to pray together. If a leaders' meeting is not held on a regular basis, it is almost guaranteed that the leaders will become discouraged and that group ministry will not flourish in the local church. Do not overlook this key ingredient. If necessary, eliminate other meetings and programs in the local church to provide time for this key element of a successful group program.

(See the end of the chapter for a sample report form to use on a monthly basis to be turned in during the leaders' meeting.)

The leadership structure

Even though your group ministry may begin very small—perhaps with only one or two groups—it is essential to organize a leadership structure from the beginning that will allow you to build and expand as the number of groups in your church grows. There is no need to be continually reorganizing.

A simple but viable staff structure is as follows:

• pastor as supporter and vision builder
• lay leader as coordinator of the overall program
• assistant lay coordinator
• coach and assistant—leaders who oversee a maximum of 10 groups each
• small-group leaders and assistants for each individual group

Note: Each of the positions listed above will always have assistant leaders who are in training.

The structure chart would look similar to this:

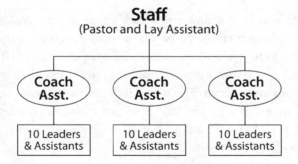

The pastor and lay member coordinator oversee the entire small-group program. The church territory is divided into sections geographically. Each coach (lay member) and assistant oversee a maximum of 10 group leaders within their assigned geographic section. The small-group leader and assistant lead a group, usually with a maximum of 12 members.

On every organizational level there will be leaders' meetings and regular contact to ensure that support and problem solving are efficient and adequate. Once the small-group support structure is in place, the pastor needs to trust the leaders to fulfill their God-given responsibilities.

How a pastor can begin a small-group ministry

1. Research. Become familiar with small-group principles through the Scriptures and church history, watch DVDs, and read books on the subject. Talk to individuals with small-group experience.

2. Attend a small-group training seminar and visit a church with an existing small-group ministry.

3. Pray and ask God to guide you to several individuals in your church with whom to share your vision for small groups. Once you have selected these persons, invite them to attend a meeting with you in which you can share your vision. The number invited should be no more than 10 individuals. An even number is best.

4. At your first meeting with these individuals, share your vision and ask them to meet one night a week for four weeks in which you will model a small group with them and spend some time teaching them small-group principles.

5. At the end of the four weeks, ask them to pray and determine if God may be asking them to be part of a small-group ministry. If they say yes, divide the group into pairs. If six individuals out of the 10 agree to be part of a small-group ministry, then once they are paired there will be three groups of two persons each. These two individuals become the leader and the assistant leader of a group. Ask these two to invite two or three other members of the church to be part of their group. Have them conduct a group for another three weeks.

6. At the end of the three weeks, meet with your group leaders and their assistants and plan with them how to begin a full-fledged group ministry to the community, using them as the beginning leaders. From these groups you will train leaders and multiply your groups.

7. Once the group ministry begins, the pastor should preach about groups and their function from the Scriptures.

8. Incorporate small-group experiences and prayer requests as part of the worship service. This will inspire and encourage others.

9. Include in the church newsletter and bulletin the dates, times, and locations of the groups and the names of the leaders, so potential members can contact them if they want to join a group.

10. Have special consecration services for the new group leaders on Sabbath morning, so the church can pray for the leaders.

11. Schedule small-group training seminars on a regular basis to train the church members.

12. Continue to have leaders' meetings to give the leaders the needed training and support.

13. Plan reaping meetings, baptismal classes, regular individual Bible studies, and other evangelistic activities to help individuals in making decisions for Jesus and the church.

14. Make small-group ministry the central part of church life and reduce the number of board meetings and other programs to provide time for the members to be involved. This is critical for the success of the ministry. People have a limited amount of time, and the church can't do everything. So choose and plan wisely for the benefit of the church members.

How a lay leader can begin a small group

1. Prayerfully study information on starting and leading groups. Pray earnestly for the leading of the Holy Spirit in seeking God's wisdom and guidance.

2. Make an appointment with your pastor. Express your desire to begin a small-group ministry in your home. Ask your pastor for counsel, help, and prayer support.

3. Attend a small-group training seminar, listen to DVDs/tapes, or read books on the topic.

4. Select a fellow church member to be your assistant leader. Meet together on a regular basis, asking God for guidance as you plan your small group.

5. If you need a place to meet other than your home, ask another member if you can use their home.

6. Make a prospect list and invite others to be a part of your group.

7. The leader and assistant leader should request a monthly meeting to inform the pastor of what is happening in the group, ask questions, and pray together.

8. As opportunities arise, share group experiences with the church members on Sabbath.

9. Recruit and train potential small-group leaders, incorporating them into the monthly meeting with the pastor.

10. Continue to pray and seek the power of the Holy Spirit as the small-group ministry grows.

I received an e-mail recently about a small-group Bible study expansion that is under way with a group of neighbors in a southern Idaho town. Susan lives in an apartment and began inviting her neighbors to her home for a small-group Bible study. The neighbors live down the hall and in a nearby mobile home park. The group members continued to invite their friends, and the group grew. Two new groups have emerged. One group leader is so excited that her group has outgrown her apartment. A local community center is their new location. Several of the group members have accepted Jesus into their lives and demonstrated their commitment and faith through baptism. Prayer, being friendly, and being an encourager will assist in growing your group, just like Susan's group.

---

*Ellen G. White, *Evangelism,* p. 125.

SMALL GROUP WEEKLY REPORT

Group _____ Area _____ Meeting date _____
Leader _____ Asst. Leader _____
Host _____ Location _____

Names of those in attendance

1. _____   11. _____
2. _____   12. _____
3. _____   13. _____
4. _____   14. _____
5. _____   15. _____
6. _____   16. _____
7. _____   17. _____
8. _____   18. _____
9. _____   19. _____
10. _____   20. _____

Please mark each name with a code: L = leader; AL = assistant leader; H = host; V = visitor; RV = return visitor; R = regular attender; M = local member; N = nonlocal member; NS = non-SDA.

Starting time for your group meeting _____ Stopping time _____

Did you use:

Praise songs? _____ Conversational prayer? _____ Empty chair? _____

Rate the quality of your group experience this week (1-10). _____ Less than 5, why? _____

Do you need to talk with the pastor? _____

Please use the back of this sheet for: (1) praise reports; (2) problem areas; (3) information pastor needs to know about yourself and people you are working with; (4) answered prayers.

Chapter 7

SMALL GROUPS 301—OFF AND RUNNING

Jennifer told me that she was scared to death the first night of her small-group meeting! She wasn't sure what to say or not say. She did not want to hurt anyone's feelings. She wanted the group to be successful. She didn't want to embarrass herself or anyone else. After much prayer and antacid for her stomach, she was ready to begin. The meeting went well, and Jennifer was off and running.

What should you say on your opening night? How do you invite someone to visit and try out the group?

Inviting a visitor

The key to a successful small group is to personally invite people with whom you are acquainted. Consider inviting neighbors, friends, work associates, relatives, your dentist, service station attendant, hairdresser, store clerk, and other general acquaintances. The invitation may take the form of a personal visit, a telephone call, or a handwritten or printed invitation. A more impersonal method is to distribute handbills advertising the types of groups available and inviting the public to call or attend a one-evening organizational meeting. Others have placed a sign in their front yard advertising the meeting.

I have found that a relaxed, nonthreatening approach is the best. Say something like this: "Sue, I'm having a small-group meeting in my home on Tuesday evenings, and I want to invite you to come try it out. Several of us are studying together the life of Jesus in the Gospels. We're looking for things to help us in dealing with everyday issues of life. I would like you to be a part of the group. Come this Tuesday night, and if you think it's for you, I'd like you to keep coming. If it doesn't meet your need for now, that's OK, too. What do you think?" Next, hand the individual a printed invitation.

Printed invitations

The following sample invitation can be set up and printed from your home computer and given to those whom you invite:

You're invited
to a small-group meeting in my home.
I hope you will be able to join us!

We will be discussing: _____

Day: _____ Time: _____

My address is: _____

Phone: _____ E-mail: _____

The next-best thing to a personal invitation is a telephone invitation. When calling a friend or neighbor on the phone, say something similar to the suggested invitation to "Sue" given above. Then follow up telephone conversations by sending a printed or written invitation via postal mail or e-mail. Experience has shown that actually mailing the invitation through the post office increases the likelihood of the person attending the small-group meeting. The reason is that the individual can actually hold something in their hand that reminds them of the meeting. Also, the extra effort shows your genuine desire for the one invited to attend.

Yard signs

Also, if you are inviting individuals who do not know the location of your home, you may want to use a yard sign to help them find the meeting site. The sign is similar to the For Sale signs used by real estate agents, and on the meeting day you can place it in your yard in the afternoon. (Check zoning requirements.) A sample yard sign might look like the following:

> **NEIGHBORHOOD**
> **HOME BIBLE STUDY**
> Tuesday - 7:00 P.M.
> *You are welcome!*

Welcome poster

Others are not comfortable placing a sign in their front yard. Instead, they print a simple poster from their home computer and tape it to their front door so that when the guests arrive, they know they are at the correct home without having to knock on the door to find out. The poster is printed on a standard-size piece of paper, and simply states:

> # WELCOME
> to Our
> Home Small Group
>
> *This is the home of*
> *Fred and Sally*

Handbills or postcards

Some churches have mailed handbills or postcards (or handed them out door-to-door) inviting people in the community to attend a small group. The invitation piece would include the topic, dates, time, and location of the small-group meeting. If this method is used, it is best to have the groups meet in several different types of locations such as homes, a schoolroom, the church fellowship hall, etc. A phone number or Web site registration needs to be made available.

As persons call the number, they should be directed to the group meeting nearest their home. As follow-up, the caller should receive a letter with details concerning the small group, plus a visit or a phone call from the group leader.

A number of years ago Bill told me this story. Bill's local church mailed a flyer advertising home small groups to every home in town. The church had set up homes to host the small-group studies along with several groups organized to meet at the church fellowship hall. The flyer indicated that the groups were sponsored by the Seventh-day Adventist Church. It seems that Bill's neighbor had an interest in the topic advertised, which was a discussion on the book of Revelation. The neighbor knew that Bill was an Adventist, so he knocked on Bill's door and handed him the flyer. The neighbor said, "Bill, are you going to have one of these groups in your home? If you do, I want to come."

Bill was somewhat taken aback by the question and responded, "Well, no, I wasn't."

The neighbor replied, "If I come, would you have a group?"

And that's how Bill became a small-group leader!

Growing your small group

Every small group needs to have evangelism as its emphasis. Otherwise, it can become a clique or a closed society that views visitors as intruders.

Here are several ways to begin new groups:

1. *Open/Empty-chair principle.* Each group should have an empty chair in its circle at each meeting. The chair should be filled at the next meeting as group members invite others to attend. Your group should pray each

week for God to lead someone to the next meeting. As the group grows by this process, it will eventually multiply and divide to form a new group. I attended a group meeting recently in which we placed an actual physical chair in the middle of our prayer circle and asked God to lead someone to our group members whom we could invite. This focuses the members' attention on considering whom they might invite.

2. *Scheduling or location conflicts.* Sometimes existing group members, or others who desire to belong to a study group, cannot attend the existing group because of scheduling or location conflicts. This means it's time to form a new group.

3. *Interests, friends, former members, etc.* Invite individuals from church interest lists, newly baptized members, visitors to church, former members, friends, work associates, and others that come to mind.

4. *Bible study students.* Invite your Bible study students to become part of a small group.

5. *Reaping meetings follow-up.* Conduct a revival or evangelistic reaping meeting and invite those attending to form small-group Bible study groups. (This is an excellent method; it works extremely well!)

6. *Begin small.* Whenever you have one person who desires to study the Bible, form a small group and invite others. Remember, two people can begin a small group! Being small is not a reason not to begin. The Holy Spirit and personal invitations will cause your group to grow.

The first night's meeting

As a leader you will probably feel some tension on your first night. This is normal, but remember that you are a child of God. He has asked you to speak for Him. Those whom God calls He also empowers. When you are empowered, God will melt away the tension and replace it with relaxation and words from Him. As a public speaker for the past 35 years, I can attest to God's victories in ministry. Here are two promises I have found helpful: "Be anxious for nothing, but in everything by prayer and supplication, with thanksgiving, let your requests be made known to God; and the peace of God, which surpasses all understanding, will guard your hearts and minds through Christ Jesus" (Phil. 4:6, 7). "For God has not given us a spirit of fear, but of power and of love and of a sound mind" (2 Tim. 1:7).

On the first night, have your assistant leader and host (if you have one) meet early with you. Once the room is prepared and the details are in order, have a season of prayer together. Basic preparation includes:

- turning on the outside houselights if it is dark outside.
- taping the welcome poster on the front door.
- arranging extra chairs in a circle.
- having extra Bibles on hand.
- having plenty of Bible study guides and extra pencils.

It is very important to make everyone feel relaxed when you begin your small-group meeting. I like to say something like this:

"I'm really glad to see each of you here tonight. As you know, this is a home small group, and we meet together for friendship, fun, and learning how the Bible can help us in our everyday lives.

"I want each of you to feel relaxed and not be on edge. Just be yourselves. You are not going to be asked to do or say anything you don't want to do or say. Some of us have never studied the Bible before, and that is OK. We all have to begin sometime. If you need help finding a chapter and verse in the Bible, I will help you. Someone had to help me when I first began. We will pray in the group, but I will pray, and later on, if some of you want to pray, that is OK too. When it comes to reading, if you like reading out loud, you can. If you don't like to read, that is fine. Some of us do, and others don't. In other words, we are all different, and we want to respect the privacy and differences of each other. How does that sound?

"Let's begin by getting acquainted with one another. I will see how good I am at remembering everyone's name. Sitting beside me is Sue. Sue is my neighbor down the street, and we have been friends for several years. Next is Dave, a longtime friend of mine. Sitting next to Dave is Tom. I met Tom last week at the grocery store. We started talking, and I invited him to stop by tonight. Next is Doris. She is a friend from work. OK, now that we have heard each other's names, let's see if you can remember them. Let's take a few minutes and see how well we do."

At this point I let the people spend a little time talking to each other and getting acquainted. Then I continue by saying,

"Next week we will talk more about what we will do in our group, but tonight I will briefly explain what we usually do. There are three basic parts to the meeting. When we begin, we have what we call *sharing time*. During this time we talk about what has happened in our lives since we last met. We also usually discuss a question that helps us to get better acquainted with one another. The second thing we do is our *study time*. In our case I am suggesting we use the study guides *Face to Face With Jesus,* along with our Bibles. There are 13 lessons in this study, so it will take us about three months to complete the study guides. Last, we talk about our personal needs or concerns, and I will lead us in *praying* for these items. As I previously mentioned, I or Dave, my assistant, will do the praying, and if some of you want to pray, you can. There is no pressure on anyone to pray. How does that sound to you? Do you have any questions or comments?

"Let's begin our meeting together tonight so you will understand better what a meeting is like. Next week we will discuss where and when we will meet, how long to meet each evening, your ideas about the meeting format, etc. I want all of us together to decide and agree about the details of our small group."

After this, begin the meeting and be ready to discuss the group agreement (covenant) at the next meeting. The first few meetings, make sure that the members are relaxed and that they feel that their input is important. The key is to pray, do your best, be friendly, and keep smiling.

The second meeting

At the next meeting, welcome everyone back. If there are any new people, introduce them to the group. Review the same thoughts you shared at the previous meeting, and then give everyone a copy of the group agreement (covenant) form to go through together. Some leaders like to discuss the details of the covenant without handing out the form, then once it has been discussed, they hand out the form and let the members fill it out. However, some leaders do not use a printed sheet at all. They simply let the group discuss the covenant and agree to it verbally.

Be sure to discuss (1) what day your group will meet, (2) the best time for the meeting, (3) how much time to spend on the three sections of sharing, Bible study, and prayer, and (4) whether preparation is expected outside of the group. Agree to call if you cannot attend the group meeting. Discuss inviting new people and the goal of multiplying the group. Also, have the members write down the name and phone number of the leader, assistant leader, and host.

Because some members of the group may not be acquainted with the Bible, explain some of the basics. Don't ask if anyone needs an introduction to the Bible; just assume someone does. Show the list of books printed in the front of the Bible, including the page number on which each book begins. Explain that the Bible is divided into the Old and New Testaments. Demonstrate how to locate a book, chapter, and verse.

After a few meetings, when the group members are fairly relaxed with one another, the group leader needs to introduce the concept of conversational prayer. Remember that public prayer makes many people nervous. They are afraid of sounding foolish, of not knowing what to say, or of being judged by others. Fear of praying will disappear as a group learns the basics of praying together. Tell your group members that no one will be pressured to pray. If a person wants to pray, they can do so. The key is to speak to God with openness of heart.

Here are several guidelines to follow in teaching your group to pray together:

1. *Model praying.* As a leader, model how to pray by praying first. After the leader prays, others will continue. Remember you might need to explain to someone what prayer is. I once visited with a woman who began sharing with me some of the problems in her life. The opportunity was there for me to pray with her. I asked if it would be OK if I prayed. She said yes. I bowed my head and began to pray. After I had spoken several words, she interrupted me. I opened my eyes, and she was looking at me with a quizzical look on her face. She said, "Kurt, what are we supposed to do when we pray? I have never prayed out loud with someone before." I explained to her how to pray, and we began again. When I finished, she said, "That is the most beautiful thing anyone has ever done for me." Don't take it for granted that everyone knows how to pray!

2. *Keeping individual prayer requests brief.* Don't spend too much time sharing prayer requests. Pray for the needs of the group. If another group member wishes to pray for the same item or need, they may do so—or they may simply say amen as the previous individual concludes their prayer.

3. Keeping it simple. Select one topic at a time as your group is learning to pray together. Some groups have a three-pronged prayer. First, the members begin by praising and thanking God in prayer. Second, they pray about needs outside the group—friends, events, situations, etc. Third, they pray for needs within the group—family, self, fellow group members, the group itself, etc.

4. The open/empty chair. The group should next pray for the "empty chair" to be filled by a new group member.

5. The Lord's Prayer. The group can conclude by saying the Lord's Prayer together. Saying the prayer together gives every group member an opportunity to pray. Many members will not know the Lord's Prayer. Printed copies should be made available for each member.

(For further help and ideas regarding prayer in small groups, see Chapter 5, "Small Groups 101—The Basics.")

Problems in groups

Wouldn't it be nice if life were trouble-free! Small groups are like families, and sometimes there are conflicts, just as there are in families. In the group, members share about themselves how they are feeling, the issues of life that are causing both positive and negative experiences, and their need for caring, understanding, and support. When you bring varied personalities together on a regular basis, there is bound to be some conflict.

A while back the telephone rang: it was my pastor friend Dave. Dave told me that some of the group leaders in his church wanted help in dealing with conflicts between group members and advice on how to keep the group on track. He had shared some ideas, but he and the group leaders felt a leaders' meeting on the topic would be helpful. A few weeks later I met with him and his group leaders, and we had an excellent discussion together.

Almost every problem in a group arises from six areas of group life. These areas are expectations of group members, participation of members in group life, the content of the meeting, the group leader's leadership skills, following the details of the group covenant, and the interaction of the members. Here are some of the ideas and concepts we discussed that night with Pastor Dave and his group leaders.

1. *Expectations.* Every member of a group has expectations of what the group should be like. Those expectations are reflected in what they perceive to be the group's purpose, the benefits they should receive personally, what they have to offer the other group members, and how the leader should conduct the group. If these issues are not discussed in the first few weeks of group life, the group is setting itself up for conflict. A group agreement will help to solve these issues.

2. *Participation.* Because every person is at a different stage of growth all through life, and because issues of daily life cause a positive and negative effect upon those various stages, group members may be a support or a challenge to the leader. Most groups will have some individuals who are challenges. A normal group may include members who are quiet, highly verbal, aggressive, academic: jokesters, doubters, counselors, counselees— and one who appears to be sleeping most of the time! (You could probably add to this list.) Each of these individuals can frustrate the group and its leader now and then. For example, a person who has something to say on every topic will probably be analyzed by the group's "counselor personality," as well as causing most of the members to wish he or she wouldn't talk so much. The group leader should point out that the group members will be different from one another and that they need to be respectful and accepting of one another.

3. *Content.* Sociologists tell us that there are four basic learning styles. There are those who believe that the core of the group should be fellowship. Others believe that studying should be the group's focus. Still others will want the group leader to function as a teacher, depending on them for the group's success. Finally, the action-oriented people will be frustrated by sitting in a circle and talking. Because expectations differ, the group should discuss these four areas and agree on what is an acceptable balance in the group meeting. It is the leader's responsibility to remind the group to assist them in keeping the group on track.

4. *Leadership.* Depending on the Holy Spirit is the number one prerequisite of a group leader. However, not understanding group dynamics or being unaware of—or ignoring—issues that are causing conflict can hamper the Spirit's effectiveness. Every group leader should make it a priority to read a few books on group dynamics or attend a training seminar. In addition, being an assistant leader or participating as a group member before

becoming a group leader will go a long way toward making life easier for the leader.

It is essential for the group leader to deal with obvious conflict in the group. The sooner conflict is dealt with, the healthier the group will be. The leader needs to talk to individuals outside of the group if necessary and let the group discuss the issues. Group members need to be able to say "I am sorry," and they need to be able to say and live the statement "You are forgiven." Conflict in a group has to be dealt with sooner or later. It will eventually destroy a group, and then the members have to deal with the pieces, so why not deal with conflict as soon as it arises?

All groups go through growth stages, similar to a child growing up or to a new Christian growing in spiritual life. These stages are birth (infant), child (toddler), youth (learning life), and adult (mature understanding and accepting). If the leader and members understand these stages of growth and bonding, it assists them in understanding one another. For example, one member may still be in the child stage of Christian growth, while another is in the adult stage, and the way they relate to the group will reflect their growth stage.

5. *Group agreement (covenant)*. If a group does not have a covenant, or if the covenant is not followed by the group, then there is sure to be trouble. For example, suppose someone is a sporadic attendee and the group never knows if this person is coming to the meeting. If the members have agreed to call the leader if they are to be absent, then the leader can gently remind the offender of the agreement. If a group has a tendency to spend more time on the sharing segment of group life than agreed upon, then the leader has leverage to keep them on track; otherwise, the group needs to change its agreement.

The covenant gives authority and permission for the leader to lead the group. Without it, there is no group ownership of the details of group life, and the leader and members may become frustrated.

6. *Group interaction*. The group leader will not be able to control the way the members think or act toward one another. Individuals with chronic problems or those who dominate the group negatively may put a wet blanket over the positive interaction of the group. The leader needs to be aware of the way the members relate to each other and, if necessary, deal with the negative. Always have the group pray for one another and for their group relationships during every prayer time.

Problem solving

Neal McBride suggests a four-step strategy in dealing with problems that I have found helpful.* It is not profound, but it works!

1. *Recognition* of the problem by the group. For example, the leader or a member can say, "I sense you are upset." Or "We need to deal with this difference of opinion." Let the person or persons talk about it. The group members need to make sure that the final solution is a win/win whenever possible. The members must learn to disagree and still love and respect one another.

2. *Personalization* of the problem. Let the group understand that difficulties are normal and that it is the group's issue too, because the group is family. Whenever possible, the leader should put everyone at ease and assist the group in solving the problem together as a unit without blaming anyone in particular.

3. *Clarification* of the problem. The problem needs to be discussed and the issue clarified. Sometimes the problem is camouflaged by actions or reactions that are simply smoke screens.

4. *Resolution* of the problem. Select the best alternatives and put them into action.

Here are some typical problems small groups encounter and some suggested solutions to them.

The chronic problem person. Some individuals have problems that they cannot seem to overcome, and their continual raising of the issue disrupts the group process. The solution is to assist the individual in receiving professional assistance or to place the person in a group that deals with the issues he or she is struggling with.

A new person joins the group. A new person who has not journeyed with the group can feel as though he or she doesn't belong. In addition, the other members may no longer share as openly as they did previously. The solution is to take time in the new person's first two meetings and allow everyone to tell "their story," so that everyone is better acquainted. If the new person never seems to fit, the group leader should talk to him or her privately and say, "I sense you are not comfortable in the group." Or "Are you comfortable in the group?" Allow the person to express their feelings. It may be necessary to assist them in joining another group.

A member verbally attacks another's comments. The leader should interrupt tactfully and affirm the right to disagree, but remind everyone to be kind and respectful of one another. Talk about the issue with a smile on your face.

A group member is constantly negative. The leader or other members can talk to the person about the problem outside of the group.

Side discussions. If two members are always making comments to one another that no one else can hear, the leader should talk with them outside of the group or redirect their attention to the group.

The quiet participant versus the talkative one. The group must always respect the personalities of the members, but the group also needs to be reminded from time to time that there should be opportunity for everyone to talk. Sometimes, simply looking at a quiet person can encourage them to talk. I have discovered that the best solution for the talkative person is for the leader to take that person aside and tell them that both you and they enjoy talking and that you want them to assist you in getting others involved. Discuss possible approaches and enlist the person's assistance.

Many other issues may—and do—come up in small groups from time to time. But these suggestions should help the group to handle most problems. The regularly scheduled leaders' meeting is a time that the group leaders and pastor can discuss in depth these issues and support one another.

Dave and Sally have been small-group leaders in their church for almost six years. The group was originally started following a Revelation Seminar in their church. Some members of the church had a vision that a small group would be perfect for nurturing the newly baptized members and to continue studying with those who had not yet made decisions. Dave agreed to be the leader, and the rest is history. Two individuals were baptized as a result of the group's first year of meeting. The group continues to meet with the goal of reaching the unchurched.

Dave says that with a busy schedule, it is easy to become simply nurture-centered and to neglect to keep on inviting to the group those who are not church members. However, once the members of a group help someone to accept Jesus and be baptized, they want that experience to continue! If Dave's group can make it in spite of the members' busy lifestyles, then you and I can do the same.

---

*Neal McBride, *How to Lead Small Groups*, p. 104.

Chapter 8

COMMONLY ASKED QUESTIONS

As I have conducted small-group seminars over the years, certain questions arise repeatedly. Here are some of the most commonly asked questions.

1. I don't want anyone smoking in my house, but one of the group members smokes. What should I do?

There are several successful approaches to take in this situation. The easiest is to have a five-minute break just prior to the Bible study time. One or two individuals can accompany the smokers outside and chat with them while they are smoking. This approach also prevents interruptions during the study.

The second approach is to have an understanding that if group members can't wait for the break, but must smoke during the group meeting, they should get up and go out on the porch and then return. The problem with this approach is that it focuses attention on the individuals and may embarrass them so that they won't return. Also, they might have to leave during a vital part of the discussion.

2. Is it necessary to serve food at each meeting?

Some small-group instructors believe that food is an important ingredient of every meeting, because it is an excellent social icebreaker. However, experience has shown that small groups can be very successful without food. In fact, serving food can be a negative in some cases. Weekly preparation can become a chore, and not everyone will be able to supply the same quality of food each week. In addition, there is always the risk of a group member's feelings being hurt if others choose not to eat food that he or she has brought, because of health or religious convictions. A treat and drink is usually a safe decision.

It is appropriate to occasionally have a simple meal (soup, salad, bread) or a treat if it is a group member's birthday or another special event. If you ask the group members to bring food, make sure the group has bonded and the members are comfortable bringing food; otherwise, provide the food. You do not want to offend anyone. (Acts 2:46 mentions food as part of the home meeting.)

3. Should an offering be taken in a home-group meeting? Who pays for the group's study guide booklets?

My response, personally, is "Never take up an offering!" It is inexpensive to conduct a home meeting. Study guides for six to eight members will cost only a few dollars. I've found it to be very awkward to ask for an offering from six people whom you have invited to your home. However, some groups have told me that members have offered to pay for their own study booklets after the first booklet is completed. If finances are a difficulty, ask your local church for assistance. Almost every church has a budget for Bible study materials.

4. What is the pastor's role in small groups in the local church?

The pastor's leadership and support in the process of organizing small groups and their ongoing functions is the difference between success and mediocrity. Although it is true that small-group leadership and participation is the responsibility of the church members, the involvement of the pastor is *vitally necessary.*

The pastor should provide the following leadership ingredients:

* Publicly share, with the church members, personal convictions concerning the importance of small groups.
* Preach a sermon or a series of sermons on the biblical basis and necessity for small-group meetings.
* Provide time in church on Sabbath for the members of small groups to share their experiences. This will inspire others to want to become involved.
* Meet regularly with the small-group leaders. At this meeting, the pastor should: pray with and for the group members; answer questions they may have; allow the leaders to share their positive and negative experiences; provide background information and helpful suggestions regarding the study guide if the groups are all using the same material; and provide resource suggestions.

- Keep accurate, up-to-date records concerning the spiritual development of the members attending the groups.
- Provide (or arrange for) training on visitation and follow-up, making decisions, and other necessary soul-winning skills.
- Provide ongoing training and mentoring of small-group leaders.

Some pastors have found success with a small-group fair. The suggestion is to have a church service centered upon the church's small-group ministries. Set up tables in the church foyer or fellowship hall with existing small-group leaders at the tables. Let them share details about their existing or planned group and invite the church members to become part of their group.*

5. Is it possible to modify small-group study guide materials so that they can be used in a classroom style of teaching?

Although small-group study material is designed to be used in the small-group home setting, some individuals have successfully used these materials in a classroom environment. If you find yourself in a situation best served by a classroom style but want to use small-group materials, provide a room in which individuals can sit in groups around tables or place the chairs in circles or sit in pews in sections of the sanctuary but clustered in groups.

In such a setting the leader will guide the entire teaching process from the front of the room. The leader gives an introduction to the lesson and then has the members share the interaction questions in their small group. If the class members are not in individual clusters, then the leader can ask for volunteers to share with the entire group.

A better way, however, is for the class members to share with the person sitting next to them. The leader guides the Bible study with the entire group, but periodically he or she has class members share with the person sitting next to them—or if the class is in clusters, the members can share among themselves, or the sharing can come from volunteers within the entire group.

Because the study guide is being used in a large group, the leader may not know how the group members are responding individually to the subject matter. Also, the leader will have no way to hear or respond to the discussion concerning a person's response to accepting Jesus or a particular doctrine. Consequently, an organized visitation program to determine the interest of the individuals is essential. During the visit, answer questions and offer reading material dealing with subjects of interest. At the meeting, decision cards may be used.

If the classroom method is used, remember to provide a warm, nonthreatening atmosphere. Otherwise, your attendance will usually decrease.

6. What are some suggestions for handling an overly talkative member?

A few suggestions have been given earlier in this book; however, here are a few more pointers gleaned from experienced small-group leaders:

- Establish the rule that a person can speak only once on a given topic, unless everyone else who wants to speak has had a chance.
- Establish a rule of no interrupting.
- Although I prefer to let members respond spontaneously, if one member causes a serious problem by monopolizing the conversation it may be best to "go around the circle" in letting people respond to questions. Once a question is asked and someone responds, then systematically go around the circle, allowing others either to speak or pass.
- If you know your group members well, you can direct a question to a particular member. However, be careful not to embarrass anyone.

7. What are some suggestions for handling someone who believes he or she has the "final answer" on most topics?

- Kindly thank the person for their answer and then ask the rest of the members how they feel about the topic. Say, "I appreciate your answer. Here is how I understand this scripture." Share your thoughts, then ask, "What do the rest of you think about this?"
- Talk to the "answer person" outside of the meeting and tell them how much you appreciate them and their answers. Tell the person that you need their help in trying to involve other group members in the discussion. In other words, don't view the talkative person or the person with strong opinions as a negative. The goal is to get the group members to talk; some people just need encouragement. Make sure everyone gets an opportunity to speak.

- In some cases the "answer person" may need to join another group in order to "fit" the group mix. Sometimes the issue is a mismatch between the biblical knowledge and life experience of one person and that of the others. Some individuals are comfortable in this type of situation, and others are not.

8. How long should the meeting last?

The answer to this question depends on the schedule of those involved. If your group meets during lunchtime at your office, then you probably have about 30 minutes. If it meets in someone's home in the evening, then I would not go over 90 minutes. The time to begin and the length of the meeting should be agreed upon by the group members. If the agreed-upon time is violated, your group members may not return.

9. How should a group respond to a crisis during the meeting?

- Call for professional assistance if an accident occurs or if someone in your group is in immediate physical danger, threatening suicide, threatening to harm someone, or in danger of being harmed.
- If someone brings up serious marital or child/parent issues during the meeting and continues to dwell on these, ask the person to stay behind after the meeting and then try to determine how you can help. If the person is distraught during the meeting, have the assistant leader and a member of the same sex as the distraught person take them into another room and try to help. In some cases it may be appropriate for the entire group to try to support the individual. Always contact your pastor for assistance.
- Remember: *Do not try to serve as a professional counselor.* Your group exists for spiritual support and friendship. It is not a counseling service, unless you have a specific group for this purpose staffed by professional counselors. Even then, because of liability issues, you need to be careful and work with your pastor before establishing this type of group.
- In summary, your small group is there to provide love, support, encouragement, prayer, etc. Professional counseling is not your role, and you should direct those in need of such professional services to your pastor or the individual designated by your local church to handle these issues.

10. Should I write my own study material or use prepared small-group study guides?

My suggestion is that beginning group leaders use prepared study guides. I have written a number of Bible study guides on such topics as prayer, the life of Jesus, personal needs, doctrinal studies, etc. These are available through Adventist Book Centers and include:

- *Peace Is an Inside Job,* Review and Herald Publishing Association, 1995.
- *PrayerWorks,* Review and Herald Publishing Association, 1993, 2001.
- *LifeLine,* booklets 1 and 2, Review and Herald Publishing Association, 1995.
- *Face to Face With Jesus,* Review and Herald Publishing Association, 1998.
- *Focus on Prophecy* (studies in Daniel and Revelation), Voice of Prophecy, 2000.

There are numerous other study guides on Bible topics and other felt need issues by other authors.

11. My group members seem not to be bonding well with me or with each other. It weakens our meeting. I am doing everything I know how to do to conduct a good meeting. What can I do?

The answer to this question begins with a question: Would you prefer to attend a worship service that runs smoothly but in which no one was real friendly to you, or to get together with some friends in a run-down restaurant and enjoy your time together? The answer is obvious. Almost everyone would opt to spend time with their friends. Therein lies the answer to this question.

It is more important for group members to spend time together both during the meeting and outside of it, becoming genuine friends, than it is to make sure that every *i* is dotted and *t* is crossed in following the meeting program outline. People, not content, should be the focus of the group meeting. Both are important, of course; don't misunderstand. But friends enjoy getting together, and if a small group doesn't sparkle on a particular evening as much as it may have on a previous evening, that's OK. Your friends will give you a break and come back.

So if the group lacks warmth and spontaneity, invite a member home for lunch or go shopping or take a hike together. For a couple of meetings, have a longer sharing time. Have some "get acquainted" questions, such as: "Where you were born and raised?" "What was your favorite game as a child?" "What do you like to do for relaxation?"

Review chapter 11, "A Biblical Reflection on Leadership." The concepts of servant leadership and shepherd leadership presented there are significant. These two leadership lifestyles are not just theory; they are vitally necessary for a successful small group. Theory can be taught, but relationships are lived out. Your small-group members can detect the difference. So if you have the theory and technique down and the group is still sluggish, it is time to warm up the group by warming up your heart and home!

12. How do I find and train new leaders?

See Chapter 13, "Developing Small-Group Leaders."

13. What is the number one essential in the success of a small group?

The answer is one word: *prayer*. "And when they had prayed, the place where they were assembled together was shaken; and they were all filled with the Holy Spirit, and they spoke the word of God with boldness" (Acts 4:31).

14. Should we provide child care or a spiritual program for the children of our group members?

The greatest gift we can give anyone is the knowledge about Jesus Christ and the plan of salvation. Teach the children about Jesus; don't simply provide child-care services. Group leaders can usually find someone in the church willing to assist with the children. Use materials prepared specifically for children to provide them with a biblically stimulating, life-changing experience. Vacation Bible School materials are excellent. If the kids enjoy the small group, the parents will be back—guaranteed. It has been said, "If you take a child by the hand, you will take the parent by the heart."

There are some small groups, especially those made up of young couples with children, who enjoy keeping the children with the adults for a portion of the meeting. Also, this is a way of modeling family worship for young families who may never have had a good model of effective family worship.

15. *Where can I find published small-group materials written by Adventist authors?*

Small-group materials and study guides on various topics are available from Adventist Book Centers and on www.adventistbookcenter.com.

16. *What should a church do to ensure that individuals do not use the small group as a place to carry out their own agenda; be divisive against the organized church; or introduce questionable material?*

All small-group leaders and all materials should be approved by the church board or designated committee or individuals. The local church should share with the church members in print through the church bulletin, newsletters, Web site, bulletin boards, etc., a list of the approved small groups, names of the leaders, and contact information. Keep the list updated. If groups or individuals with purposes "counter to the local church" create difficulties, then the local church should address the situation quickly in as kind a way as possible. If left alone, it can significantly disrupt or destroy your small-group ministry.

---

*David Livermore, the personal ministries director for the Upper Columbia Conference, Spokane, Washington, has used this method successfully.

Chapter 9

THE SEVEN LAST WORDS OF SMALL GROUPS

In 1973 Ralph Neighbor published his book on church life and ministry titled *The Seven Last Words of the Church*. Many readers of the book may not remember much about its content, but everyone remembers the title! It is a great title, and the seven last words it refers to are, of course: *We've never tried it that way before.*

One of my first experiences with the thinking behind this phrase occurred during my initial year as a conference departmental director. I was in a planning meeting of local conference personal ministries directors. The chairperson was leading a discussion on the topic of how to resurrect the church's community fund-raising campaign known as "Ingathering." The core issue was that church member involvement was falling every year, and something had to be done about it or no one would be doing Ingathering.

Ideas past and present were freely discussed—mainly ideas from the past as gray-haired gentlemen (I can say that, because I'm now in that category myself!) waxed eloquent about successful methods of bygone days. One recalled strapping loudspeakers to the roof of his car and playing Christmas carols as church members knocked at the door of every house in town. Another described standing at the door holding a round, can-shaped container with a built-in crank (like a child's jack-in-the-box toy). As he turned the crank, the device played Christmas music to accompany his appeal for funds. Then there was what I called the "blitzkrieg method," in which the pastor rallied church members to form caroling bands and go door-to-door in marathon sessions that accomplished the work in four nights rather than two or three weeks. This was my method of choice in the churches in which I was pastor.

Now, I am not being negative about these methods. In fact, they still work in some parts of the world. The issue was that in North America, at the time of this discussion, they were not working. There was nothing wrong with some of the methods—except for the fact that for many church members and pastors in North America, they were simply no longer culturally relevant.

I listened to the discussion for a long time and then innocently raised my hand. All eyes turned to look at me, waiting for the young "new kid on the block" to make his first speech. "Rather than rehash old methods," I suggested, "why not pretend like we are starting Ingathering for the first time? Based on the purpose and the desired results, let's ask the question 'What methods would we use if we were beginning this program today?' If some of the methods of the past fit today's society, let's use them. If not, let's replace them with new methods."

There was deafening silence. The chairperson looked at me and literally did not respond. After about 10 seconds (it seemed like 15 minutes to me), he looked away, ignored my comment, and went on with his original discussion. Later someone told me that the chairperson had decided I was a "rebel." (The "rebel" in me says he should have listened. When was the last time your local church made Ingathering a December church ministry priority?)

In essence, I was being told, "We have never done it that way before." The discussion was over.

There is a paradox about the way God works with men and women involved in ministry. God's ways are always old *and* new. God states, "Do not remember the former things, nor consider the things of old. Behold, I will do a new thing" (Isa. 43:18, 19). And then, only three chapters later, we read: "Remember the former things of old, for I am God, and there is no other" (Isa. 46:9).

I believe there is an ongoing, creative tension between the old and the new in how God carries out His plans. We must always live on the cutting edge of the ways of God. Times move on, and the five-inch-wide necktie of one era moves over for the two-and-a-half-inch necktie of another era. Neckties are still in style, but the way they are displayed changes almost as often as the seasons.

In the world of religion, too, the issues are basically the same from generation to generation, but the words we use and the approaches we take to address them change. Both the Athenians of Acts 17 and the postmoderns of today are worshippers of the "unknown god." The long-haired "hippie" of the sixties was searching for meaning in life, just the same as was the "rich young ruler" of Luke 18 or the 28-year-old of today with his buzz-cut hairstyle. As the words of the song state, "the God of the mountain is the God of the valley." And the God of Genesis is still the Savior of the Gospels and the coming King of Revelation. You see, all people are created to be perfectly whole only through Jesus Christ, and the deceiver of Genesis in the Garden of Eden is still the great deceiver of Revelation and the destroyer of people in our day.

In order to be relevant to the times in which we live, we must always be people of both the old and of the new. As we explore how to "do church" and "how to live out small groups" in our day, we must be open to what God has offered throughout the ages. Remember, He is God and says, "I am the Lord, I do not change" (Mal. 3:6).

Using old methods in new contexts

It is time to reexamine where we have been with small groups and where God wants us to go from here. We must blow off the dust from certain tried-and-true principles and begin to re-implement them, using contemporary methods. Ellen White, in the book *Evangelism*, put it this way: "Men are needed who pray to God for wisdom, and who, under the guidance of God, can put new life into the old methods of labor and can invent new plans and new methods of awakening the interest of church members and reaching the men and women of the world."[1]

It is obvious that something has to change if we are going to finish the work on this earth. It is interesting to me that Lyle Schaller, a highly respected author and church consultant in mainline Protestant churches, reflected Ellen White's sentiments when he said, "The old wineskins of denominations will not make it into the next millennium."[2] Schaller is referring to the lack of lay involvement in church ministry, and the millennium he referred to is now—the millennium that began with the twenty-first century. The article continues: "Today, equipping is more than a spiritual gifts seminar or a volunteer management program. It's not a program at all, but a whole paradigm shift in church leadership."

These statements of Lyle Schaller and Ellen White regarding the involvement of church members in ministry is as relevant as when God had the apostle Paul write about it in 1 Corinthinas 12 and Ephesians 4. The message of these texts is that God created each person with a unique set of talents and gives each of us Spirit-endowed gifts to serve others and tell them the story of Jesus. My experience is that Christians want to serve others; some just need inspired leadership to guide the way. They need a mentor, an encourager. In other words, *no more business as usual*. As Seventh-day Adventists, we have had for many years the counsel that church growth consultants are now calling "new wineskins" and "paradigm shifts." They are saying that the lay leadership of the church will be actively involved in a team ministry that makes them producers, not just spectator Christians. It is time for Seventh-day Adventists to move ahead by example and action. We have the counsel; why not take the lead?

Notice the balance reflected in Ellen White's statements in this area: "There must be no fixed rules; our work is a progressive work, and there must be room left for methods to be improved upon. But under the guidance of the Holy Spirit, unity must and will be preserved."[3] "Means will be devised to reach hearts. Some of the methods used in this work will be different from the methods used in the work in the past; but let no one, because of this, block the way by criticism."[4]

Remember this point: Methods change, but standards and doctrines are not negotiable! As Seventh-day Adventists, we have the unique messages of the three angels of Revelation 14 to share with the inhabitants of the world. That's a nonnegotiable item. However, we must continually look for new and contemporary ways to share those messages without compromise.

How do these changes in methods impact the application of small groups? First, all biblically based small groups have the Acts 2 ingredients as part of the group experience, and second, the way in which the Acts 2 ingredients are applied may differ from culture to culture and circumstance to circumstance. Just as there have always been various small-group models, there will be more models in the future!

The Old and New Testament principles of Christian community and church life are part of the nature of Jesus Himself. They are changeless. It is the concept of new wine in old wineskins (Matt. 9:17). The "wine" (the substance) does not change, but the container (the structure) does. However, the container is still a container, just as the wine is still wine!

Regarding the principle of "new wine into old wineskins" (verse 17), I have experienced drinking Communion grape juice ("fruit of the vine"

Mark 14:25) from long-stemmed glassware, one-ounce plastic or glass containers, a pewter goblet, and a paper cup. What this means is that the Communion grape juice can be poured into many different types of drinking
containers. The basic requirement of all containers is to contain the wine.
However, glasses (containers) may be plastic, paper, wood, metal, or crystal.
Containers come in many different shapes, sizes, and colors. What is important is that it is able to contain liquid. The container may change, but the
basic design, nature, and use remain the same.[5]

I am excited as I think about God's desire for your church and mine—
an empowered lay movement of individuals using their ministry gifts in
glorious harmony for the purpose of reaching unchurched people for Jesus.
A key way to make this happen is through a vibrant small group in your
home, at your place of business, or a local restaurant.

Society has changed since my first exposure to small groups back in
1970. The organizational approach to these groups and their agendas and
content have changed—and well they should. If your small-group thinking
and approach hasn't moved with the changing times, then consider why it
should.

Changes in society

Think about the changing dynamics of American society. In 1940 only
28 percent of American women—approximately one fourth—were in the
workforce. Between 1950 and 1970 the number of working *mothers* in the
United States nearly doubled. By 1970 more than 25 percent of mothers
with children under 6 years of age were in the labor force. This statistic has
kept pace with the growing population.[6] In 1997 women comprised nearly
half of the workforce, with 46.6 percent. This dramatic increase of women
working outside the home has changed not only the job environment but
the family model as well, creating today's culture of the working mother.[7] In
fact, companies have made numerous adjustments to accommodate mothers in the workplace—flexible hours, the ability to work part-time, family
leave, on-site day care, and other amenities that were unheard-of 25 years
ago.[8]

The era of the working mom has also caused a shift in the role of fathers. The days of the stay-at-home mom allowed the 9:00-to-5:00 dad to
have an evening with his buddies during the week or more time for church

ministry. But surveys of fathers 20 to 30 years of age suggest that they are taking an active and equal role in raising children, doing housework, and fixing meals. A study by the Families and Work Institute found that fathers today spend one more hour a day with their children than fathers did 25 years ago![9] This is a significant statistic when it comes to "Dad's" availability in involvement in church life.

Even the makeup of the family has changed. In 1950, 5.9 percent of all households had four or more children—compared to only 1.9 percent of households in 1998. The average family today has one or two children.

We even heat our homes differently. In 1950 more than 34 percent of all households heated the home by coal, with 27 percent using gas or electricity. Forty years later, in 1990, more than 75 percent of all U.S. households used gas or electricity as the main source of home heating. Only 0.4 percent of households used coal.[10]

In 1950 a one-car garage was all that was needed. By 1970, as more women entered the workplace and more funds were available to the average household, another car was added to the family—along with the double-car garage. In 2010 a three- or even four-car garage is common. Today, not only do mom and dad each have a car, but in numerous households, so do each of the kids.

All these lifestyle shifts mean that parents today have much fewer hours in a day or a week to contribute to local church ministry compared to the typical parent of 25 years ago. Not only has "free time" disappeared, but perceptions of personal needs are somewhat different.

With dads spending more time with children and household chores, and with the dramatic increase in the number of women in the workplace, available volunteer hours have diminished markedly. Because more mothers with young children are in the workplace, they are not able to get the household and family chores done during the day as in the past. This means that both mothers and fathers are caring for these home responsibilities during hours they used to spend being involved in church life.

Instead of decrying these facts of contemporary society, we must shift with them. From a small-group perspective, this means that a family in which both the husband and wife work outside the home might not have time in the schedule each week for a small-group meeting, church attendance, and other church responsibilities. In addition, the topics discussed in a small group might need to reflect the issues created by their lifestyle.

For example, the small group might meet every other week rather than weekly. The topics within the Bible study might include scripturel-based discussions on parenting, working moms, and coping with stress in today's society. In other words, people want the Bible and God to be relevant to their needs. If your small group fulfills a need, the people will come; if needs are not met, they will do something else. Time is of the essence for them. They will vote with their feet.

This all means that a "one-way-fits-all" approach to small groups will not be as effective today as in the past. There is no single (model) way to "do" small groups. In summary here are 10 key core values of small-group ministry, as I see it.

Ten core values of small groups

1. Each member must accept for themselves Jesus' prayer of oneness, which is a Spirit-filled life that makes one a fully devoted disciple of Jesus Christ.

2. Members of a church must see themselves as one body (see 1 Cor. 12), or they won't care about the person sitting across the aisle at church or living next door.

3. A large-group experience and a small-group experience must be available for all church members.

4. Small groups must mobilize all church members to ministry service and be an experience that is driven by spiritual gifts. This leads an individual to become a fully devoted disciple of Jesus Christ.

5. A small group must include spiritual growth and soul winning (outreach) in order to be biblical. A small group is central to the evangelism process of the local church.

6. The small-group agenda arises from Scripture.

7. Everything the church does must include small-group DNA.

8. A small group should be culturally relevant.

9. One must actively choose/commit to be a part of those who make small groups successful.

10. No one cares for more people than their life schedule allows, but everyone is cared for.

---

[1] Ellen G. White, *Evangelism*, p. 105.

[2]Lyle Schaller, *Net Fax,* Apr. 1, 1996, p. 1. Quoted in *Current Thoughts and Trends,* June 1996, p. 3.

[3]Ellen G. White, *Evangelism,* p. 105.

[4]*Ibid.*

[5]William Beckham, *Where Are We Now?,* pp. 17, 18.

[6]Seth Low and Pearl J. Spindler, "Child Care Arrangements of Working Mothers in the United States."

[7]Teena Rose, "Working Moms Carve Out Their Own Office Space."

[8]*Ibid.*

[9]*Ibid.*

[10] Demographics of the U.S.: Trends and Projections Report, "Households by Presence and Number of Children Under Age Eighteen, 1950 to 1998."

SECTION II:
SMALL-GROUP LEADERSHIP

Chapter 10

A SMALL-GROUP LEADER—
WHO, ME?

My dog's name was Heidi, a mutt by birth and part chicken when frightened. My dad had a booming voice that would send Heidi cowering behind the nearest shrub when he scolded her for digging a hole in the lawn. You would think her life was over, the way she trembled.[1]

The Bible tells us that Saul had a similar experience. Chosen by God to lead the nation, Saul instead went to hide among the pots and pans near the KP tent. We read the story in 1 Samuel 10:17-27. God sent Samuel to establish Saul as king of Israel, but when the people looked for him, Saul could not be found. God told them he was hiding among the "equipment" and that they should go get him (verse 22). The people dragged Saul from his hiding place by the scruff of the neck, and there he stood—the new king, shaking in his sandals—afraid, but ready to be used by God. Saul was clueless about how to lead the people. Verse 25 states that Samuel explained to Saul and the people how a king was supposed to act and lead.

Maybe that is how you feel about being a small-group leader. Maybe you feel God tugging at your heart or your fellow group members urging you to be a leader. But your legs are trembling, and your heart is pounding, and you prefer to melt into the background. One thing I know—when God calls you, He will be right there helping you to accomplish what He asks you to do. God does not make mistakes. So step forward and let God use you mightily for Him. Your small group will be blessed, and so will you!

Remember this: Because we are human, no one can perfectly meet all the standards of leadership. We are perfect only in Jesus Christ. When we look at the characteristics of a leader, no one measures up. So don't be discouraged. If the desire of your heart is to possess these leadership characteristics, and if you are committed to growing in the grace and power of

Jesus Christ, then God can use you for Him. Let's get started. If you are a small-group leader, the foundation of your leadership ministry will be your commitment to the following basic principles:

1. *An understanding of and commitment to spiritual principles.* Paul wrote that church leaders should not be novices in the Christian life (see 1 Tim. 3:6; 5:22). Spiritual leaders must themselves understand Scripture and have an experience in the things of God before they can lead others spiritually. A small-group leader's daily walk with God through Bible study and prayer is the foundation of their ministry.

2. *A growing relationship with Jesus.* If a leader is to model spiritual growth and encourage others, a growing relationship with Jesus must first be a reality in their own life. A developing Christlike character must be evident. Several times New Testament letters encourage God's children to "grow in the grace and knowledge of our Lord and Savior Jesus Christ" (2 Peter 3:18).

3. *A commitment to care for people.* A leader is dedicated to reaching out to the members of the group and demonstrating loving concern for their personal sorrows, joys, and needs. In addition, it is essential that a leader be an encourager, helping members in their personal growth and development. Jesus said that true leadership involves putting the needs of others first. The leader also models what they are teaching by being a living example—an authentic Christian.

4. *A passion for leading people to Jesus.* The number one reason for the existence of the church is to connect people with Jesus. A leader must have this burning desire.

5. *A student of the Bible.* The group leader needs to enjoy studying and learning about the Scriptures on a daily basis. A leader cannot facilitate a scriptural study if they do not study personally.

6. *A willingness to be teachable.* At first a leader may not know very much about leading a group, but if they are humble and willing to learn, they have the necessary ingredients for success. It is a must as a small-group leader (and in life) to remain teachable.

7. *A willingness to make a commitment of time.* It takes time to be a group leader. The leader must be willing to prepare for the weekly meeting, spend one day/night a week in a group meeting, make sure the members' needs are being met, and attend regularly scheduled leaders' meetings. Of course, the assistant leader and, in many cases, other group members will also help

to meet the needs of the group members outside the group time. But the leader must be willing to make a commitment of their time to the needs of the group.

There are other characteristics of a group leader, but these are the basic ones. Keep in mind that none of us meet all of these characteristics as perfectly as we would like, but Jesus has promised us strength and the power of the Holy Spirit.

Closely tied to these characteristics is the need for flexibility and a willingness to change/adapt your own personal approach to leading a small group depending on the needs of your group members. Disaster can happen when a leader is too rigid about what group life should resemble and how they should lead the group. The leader can effect change only to the extent to which they are willing to embrace changes. If you want to continue leading, then you must always be open to change. Each group dynamic is different. The group you lead today is different than your previous group; people are constantly changing and growing.

Henry Ford, founder of the Ford Motor Company, was notorious for his resistance to change. The year was 1912, and the Model T was 4 years old. Production of the Model T continued for 20 years, from 1908 to 1928, with more than 15 million automobiles produced during that time. Ford's innovative assembly-line concept was producing a new car faster than anyone had ever dreamed—in one tenth of the time required previously. The Model T eventually came in numerous body styles, but early on Henry Ford had said no to anyone wanting to make changes in what was working so successfully.

Ford's top production man, William Knudsen, could see the sun eventually setting on the idea of only a single body style, so he decided to prepare the Model T for the future. Knudsen knew that the future lay in multiple color choices and different body styles. While Henry Ford was away on an extended trip to Europe, Knudsen put his new ideas to work. When Ford returned, he visited the Highland Park, Michigan, plant and saw the new design. With outrage he "spied the gleaming red lacquer sheen on a new, low-slung version of the Model T." The car also sported four doors and a convertible top! He walked around the car three or four times and then jerked the doors off the car, ripped the convertible top, and destroyed the windshield. Ford did not want anyone messing with his one-color choice (black) and his chosen body style.

William Knudsen headed for a job with Ford's competitor, General Motors. Innovation and competition pressed in on the Ford Motor Company to the point that Henry Ford grudgingly gave in, and the Model A was born. Interestingly enough, with the birth of the Model A, Ford produced a model similar to the one Knudsen had designed that cost him his job![2]

Henry Ford believed in change—in some areas. His assembly lines, mass production methods, innovative labor relations, etc., demonstrate his leadership in this area. But in certain key areas he resisted change tenaciously. There is a lesson here for all of us as small-group leaders. Change is necessary if we are to lead effectively. The key is to be able to decide what is simply change for the sake of change and what is change in preparation for the future. We must, as Christians and as small-group leaders, encourage all people to change daily into a closer image of Jesus Christ. It is biblical to be open to change and to be a change agent.[3]

Motives for leadership

As one reflects on the characteristics for leadership in a small group, it becomes clear that the bottom line is motive. Correct motives that allow the leader to serve positively include the following:

- a desire to uplift and glorify God
- a desire to please God in using the spiritual gifts given to you
- a desire to do something positive for God's church
- a desire to share with others the fact that Christianity can meet one's personal needs
- a desire to connect non-Christian people with Jesus Christ

Incorrect motives can lead to the demise of a group and in some cases destroy the spirituality of the members. Motives that destroy group life include:

- a desire to fulfill an emotional need, such as acceptance, approval, etc.
- a desire for power or authority over others
- a desire to fulfill a personal need for approval and admiration (a "look at me" complex)
- a desire and need to be always in the center of whatever is happening

The bottom line is that the leader should desire to assist the group in reaching its goals and fulfilling its purpose for existence. If the leader's reasons for participating in the group are incorrect, they should not serve in this capacity.

If you try to use human influence or questionable, deceptive tactics and strategies to get other people to do what you want or to have them like you, then your goals for the group and yourself will not be successful in the long run. Even your positive approaches will be perceived as deceptive. If people do not trust you or view you as sincere, if they do not believe you have their best interests in mind, permanent success is not possible.

Functions of a leader

There are several functions that are basic to positive leadership. A successful group leader:

- seeks to develop personal relationships with each member of the group. This goes beyond knowing their first names and a casual "Hi, how are you?" It involves spending quality time with them and attempting to understand their unique contribution to the group.
- is sensitive to the needs, feelings, and personalities of the members, and affirms their individuality.
- continually models love, trust, and acceptance as normal behavior for Christians.
- will truly be a facilitator, guiding the flow of the discussion and attempting to involve all group members in a nonthreatening manner.
- encourages members to listen to, accept, and respect those whose views differ from the views of the leader or other members of the group.
- assists the group in accomplishing its goals and growing into a mature Christian community.

Stages or cycles of group life

- Small groups go through stages of development just as people do. It is essential that leaders understand this process. One five-stage model uses the terminology of "infant, toddler, child, youth, and adult." Another six-step model uses the terms "precontract stage, orientation stage, power and control stage, trust stage, change stage, and conclusion or new beginning stage."

However, I prefer the following terminology:

- *Exploration stage.* The members are just beginning with the group. They are asking such questions as "Do I belong?" "What is expected of me?" "What can I expect from others?"
- *Transition stage.* The members are more comfortable with one another and are beginning to venture out and "test the water" to see if the group is a safe place to belong. The members begin to relax and enjoy one another.
- *Action stage.* The group members are comfortable with one another. They are very open in sharing their personal opinions and have developed trust and acceptance within the group.
- *Termination/new beginning stage.* The group is ending, dividing into two groups. Or it is beginning a new set of study guides or establishing a new purpose for existence. The members usually feel sad that change is interrupting their established bond, but they adjust and move on to a positive new-group experience.
- Stages are a part of life. If a leader is aware of these stages and the emotions that the group members are experiencing as a result, they can talk to the group about these changes, and the members will adjust more quickly.

Leadership styles

- Understanding what is expected of you as a leader is indispensable in order for you to fulfill your job description. In addition, your attitude, methods, and behavior—that is, how you operate—will also determine your ability to facilitate a group. Let's take a look at the various leadership styles and examine which seem to be best for small-group leadership.
- Traditionally, there are four basic leadership styles. These are autocratic, authoritative, democratic, and laissez-faire.

- An *autocratic* leader is domineering and dictatorial. This type of leader tries to be in total control, with members functioning as listeners and followers. The leader determines policy and wants the group members to choose their personal goals for themselves. The autocratic leader often makes decisions unilaterally and disregards other viewpoints. The group members almost become puppets.

- An *authoritative* leader has a definite direction in mind for the group, but is open to the ideas of others. The authoritative leader usually has strong control, yet the members are actively involved in discussing the leader's goals and ideas. The leader is open to modification based on group input, but usually does not change their personal goals for the group. This type of leader uses their personal power to involve others.

- The *democratic* leader is group-centered and shares control with the group. This type of leader is assertive yet values the abilities and opinions of others. The democratic leader creates a sense of security and belonging in the group. All policies, goals, and guidelines are a matter of group discussion, and the goal of the democratic leader is group participation in and ownership of the decisions made.

- The *laissez-faire* leader is permissive and passive. This type of leader exercises minimal control. The members direct the group meeting. The leader doesn't prepare, and lets things drift. The leader appears to be passive and doesn't seem to care. This style provides fragmentation and encourages indecisiveness.

- Which of these traditional styles is best? Almost everyone would agree that each style has a place and is useful at times, but most people prefer the democratic style of leadership. However, there are two other leadership styles that need to be considered—servant leadership and situational leadership.

- The *servant leadership* style arises from Luke 22:24-30. Servant leadership is reviewed in Chapter 11, "A Biblical Reflection on Leadership." However, because of its importance, here is a brief summary.

- The disciples of Jesus were arguing about who was to be the greatest in His coming kingdom. Jesus said to them, "The kings of the Gentiles exercise lordship over them, and those who exercise authority over them are called 'benefactors.' But not so among you; on the contrary, he who is greatest among you, let him be as the younger, and he who governs as he who serves" (verses 25, 26).

- Jesus also said, "If anyone desires to be first, he shall be last of all and servant of all" (Mark 9:35). Jesus then demonstrated to the disciples what He was saying when He took the role of servant and washed their feet (see John 13:5), something the disciples evidently felt was beneath their dignity. Even though Jesus, the king of the universe, had the right to demand to be waited upon, He demonstrated that a true leader is one who earns respect and loyalty by the way they treat people. Servant leaders do not demand their own way, do not try to maneuver politically to get their own way, and, most important, do not "walk over people" or stretch the truth to accomplish their own purposes. Servant leaders put the desires and needs of others first. They earn respect because of their sincerity, commitment and honesty, love and respect of others, and a desire to build up others.

- Jesus exemplified true servant leadership when He gave His life for His followers. This is true servant leadership! The apostle Paul, in an attempt to explain this concept of being a servant, wrote: "For though I am free from all men, I have made myself a servant to all, that I might win the more; and to the Jews I became as a Jew, that I might win Jews; to those who are under the law, as under the law, that I might win those who are under the law; to those who are without law, as without law (not being without law toward God, but under law toward Christ), that I might win those who are without law; to the weak I became as weak, that I might win the weak. I have become all things to all men, that I might by all means save some" (1 Cor. 9:19-22).

- Paul was an educated man and a strong leader, but he did not demand; he served. This attitude of service does not come naturally. However, by yielding to the grace and power of Jesus Christ, we can become servant leaders who reflect the style of Jesus.

Another leadership style that has emerged in more recent discussions on the topic is what is called *situational leadership*. Situational leadership means that the style of leadership will vary depending upon the situation and circumstances. For the Christian this means that servant leadership must always be the fundamental style, but sometimes the leader is given, by per-mission of the followers, the right to be more direct when needed.

- Here is an example of situational leadership in group life. The mem-bers of one group agree to begin their meeting at 7:00 p.m. and to end at 8:30 p.m. But they always seem to start late and go overtime. This frustrates some of the members, who give the leader permission to be autocratic with the group and help them fulfill their agreement. The leader keeps the group on time, but does it with a smile on his or her face and a kind spirit.

- The choice of leadership style is key to developing a group that is enjoy-able to the members—in contrast to a group that no one wants to be-long to. In addition, a servant leadership democratic style develops new leaders. I was visiting a church and consulting with the group leaders. I was impressed with the leadership effectiveness and the personality of Sally, one of the group leaders. I asked about Sally after the meeting and was told that at one time she had been an "ECR" ("extra care required") person. Sally's attitude, insecurity, and bitterness had made those around her miserable. However, the Holy Spirit used the love, kindness, and ac-ceptance of the group members and their desire to serve Sally—to love her just as she was—to make a marked difference in her life.

Sally's story is the result of servant leadership. Because she was served, Sally now serves. That is what ministry is all about!

---

[1]Data and resources for this chapter can be found Kurt Johnson's book *Small Groups for the End Time.*

[2]Robert Lacy, *Ford: The Men and the Machine.* Story quoted by John C. Maxwell.

[3]See John C. Maxwell, *Developing the Leader Within You*, pp. 50-52.

Chapter 11

A BIBLICAL REFLECTION ON LEADERSHIP

Leadership in the Old and New Testaments— a brief summary[1]

Those who have counted state that they have discovered more than 850 definitions for "leadership" in various articles and books. Many of these definitions are from a secular perspective; others are spiritually based. A sampling of these definitions include such words as "persuade," "example," "mobilize," and "influence" as the key word of the definition.[2]

John C. Maxwell, a well-known author on the topic of leadership, has written: "Here is my favorite leadership proverb: 'He who thinks he leads, but has no followers, is only taking a walk.' If you can't influence others, they won't follow you. And if they won't follow, you're not a leader. That's the Law of Influence. No matter what anybody else tells you, remember that leadership is influence—nothing more, nothing less."[3]

No matter how many definitions one applies to leadership, "influence" is the term that summarizes the nucleus of its meaning. In fact, all other adjectives that can be used to describe leadership can be absorbed into the word "influence." This influence can take on either a positive or negative aspect.

My personal definition of small-group leadership from a Christian perspective is this: *"A leader is someone who, led by the Holy Spirit, influences others to be remade in the image of God—that is, to become a part of accomplishing God's agenda."* Yes, nothing more and nothing less.

You see, in order to be a leader you must have followers. If you are truly leading, then you are influencing your followers, by word or example, to do what you ask. I read somewhere that leadership is getting people to do what they don't want to do and yet to think that they enjoy doing it! That might be stretching the issue a bit, but the principle is valid—leaders influence people to accomplish tasks that are both pleasant and unpleasant.

In essence, everyone influences someone else. A 5-year-old influences a 3-year-old to jump in a mud puddle even though their mother told them not to. A 16-year-old encourages his 14-year-old neighbor to join his gang and follow through with the membership initiation. Or on a positive note, I recently watched a television report of a group of teens who gathered donations to develop a softball field for their community. Their long-range plan was to raise funds for charities by soliciting donations from those who use the field for free. And their plan was working—influence was at work—as the report shared the amazing willingness of the community to give because of the influence of a handful of youth.

Titles and leadership do not always mix

When people hear a person's title, they often assume that person is a leader. For example, we speak of the president of the United States or the president of General Motors. But the title does not necessarily mean that person is a leader. It may simply mean that they hold the job. Time reveals if the person is actually a leader. True leadership cannot be voted, appointed, or assigned. It must be earned. Position means nothing if the holder of the position cannot influence people positively.

History records the influence and achievements of leaders—for good or bad. Alexander the Great and Charlemagne built great empires. Gandhi achieved transformations of society through the moral influence of non-violence. Adolf Hitler influenced others to barbarianism and plunged the world into war. George Washington, Abraham Lincoln, Dwight D. Eisenhower, Margaret Thatcher, John F. Kennedy, Winston Churchill—the list is endless. No matter whom you choose to add to the list, one thing is certain: the original plan of leadership was a positive pattern first demonstrated by the Godhead.

No matter which leadership definition you choose, the bottom line is not so much your definition, but *how* you lead. Let's briefly explore leadership in the light of several biblical examples.

Redemptive leadership characteristics found in the lives of biblical leaders

There are qualities of leadership found in the lives of biblical leaders that are relevant today for us as leaders. Let's look at the following Old Testament leaders:

Moses (Heb. 11:24–29). Moses, though a man with shortcomings, demonstrated tremendous leadership traits. Hebrews 11 lists some of Moses' leadership traits—faith (verse 24), integrity (verse 25), vision (verse 26), decisiveness (verse 27), obedience (verse 28), and responsibility (verse 29). Other Bible passages describe Moses as being forgiving, having a redemptive attitude, understanding and listening to advice (see Ex. 18:15, 16; 32:32; Num. 14:11–25; Deut. 34:10).

All these traits are essential to a leader who desires to reflect God's image. Pastorally and from a church growth standpoint, several of these traits merit more consideration than others. For example, vision is essential in developing leaders in a congregation. Pastors and small-group leaders must see beyond a church member's current spiritual condition and leadership abilities and be able to visualize what that person can become in Jesus Christ.

Vision also helps the leader to set goals and objectives for the small group. Moses possessed great vision as he guided the rebellious Israelites during 40 years of wilderness wandering to achieve their goal of arriving in Canaan. Decisiveness in leadership is necessary to move a person, congregation, or small group from their current condition or situation to the desired objective. Decisiveness is a sign of strong, positive leadership.

Joseph (Gen. 37–50). Joseph is an excellent example of someone who exhibited four qualities that are important in a leader. These are:

1. moral integrity (Gen. 39:7, 8)
2. dependence on God (Gen. 41:16)
3. decisiveness (Gen. 41:33, 34)
4. organization (Gen. 41:48)

Because of his position as second in command in Egypt, Joseph had opportunity to be abusive with his authority, but he was humble while in control of the lives and destinies of people. The small-group leader does not take advantage of others, but helps improve their quality of life.

Gideon (Judges 6; 7). Gideon, a judge of Israel in the Old Testament, demonstrates three key characteristics of a leader of God. These are:

1. clarification of responsibilities (Judges 6:17)
2. obedience/faith (Judges 6:29)
3. vision (Judges 7:7)

Role clarification is an essential quality of a leader. The leader must help their followers to understand everyone's roles clearly. This is especially helpful in the beginning stages of a newly launched small-group meeting.

David (2 Sam. 5; 6). David, king of Israel, displayed several leadership characteristics that are helpful to Christian leaders:

1. recognition by others as a leader (2 Sam. 5:1)
2. diplomacy (2 Sam. 5:11)
3. crediting God for success (2 Sam. 5:12)
4. praying daily for wisdom and divine guidance (2 Sam. 5:17-25)
5. acknowledging his humanness and mistakes (2 Sam. 6:9-13)
6. leading his followers in worship (2 Sam. 6:15)

In order to lead others in spiritual growth, a Christian leader should set aside time for prayer and Bible study as David did. This is essential for personal spiritual growth and divine power. A small-group leader will personally model spiritual growth as well as mentor the group members in their spiritual-growth journey.

Elijah (1 Kings 17-19). Elijah, an Old Testament prophet, exemplifies at least two leadership qualities to consider:

1. personal daily applications of the Word of God (1 Kings 17:5)
2. dependence on God (1 Kings 19:4)

It is especially easy for strong leaders to have confidence in themselves rather than in God. A daily surrender of self to God is essential to being a humble, usable leader. Leaders are busy people, and busy people don't always slow down. Small-group leaders, in order to be effective, must slow down so they can listen to God speaking to them through Bible study, prayer, meditating on scriptures, and other means.

Leaders and their use of authority

As we consider the biblical leaders discussed above, it is obvious that they all possessed authority. Without authority, it is impossible to lead others. However, it is important to understand that "authority" and "authoritarianism" are two different things. Healthy authority is sensitive to the needs and thinking of others while striving for the good of the organization, group, or purpose. Chester Barnard, a noted author on management, states: "A person can and will accept a communication as authoritative only when four conditions simultaneously exist: (a) he can and does understand the communications; (b) at the time of his decision he believes it is not inconsistent with the purpose of the organization; (c) at the time of his decision, he believes it to be compatible with his personal interest as a whole; and (d) he is able mentally and physically to comply with it."[4]

As we reflect on leadership in the Old Testament, it is obvious that in God's plan authority flows from the higher levels to the lower levels. Of course, God is the ultimate authority, utilizing human beings as instruments to accomplish His purposes.

Moses set up lines of authority following Jethro's advice (see Ex. 18:13-27). The Aaronic priesthood was organized with a high priest at the top and orders of priests under him in varying ranks (see 1 Chron. 24). In rebuilding Jerusalem, Nehemiah established a line of command (see Neh. 3-6). A successful leader will have authority over others, but this authority will be earned rather than imposed. His authority will be positive, but not abusive.

The following Bible passages demonstrate God's search for leaders. The key to spiritual leadership is to ask regarding all decisions and actions: "Am I glorifying God?"

"The hand of the diligent will rule, but the slothful will be put to forced labor" (Prov. 12:24).

"For exaltation comes neither from the east nor from the west nor from the south. But God is the Judge: He puts down one, and exalts another" (Ps. 75:6, 7).

"So I sought for a man among them who would make a wall, and stand in the gap before Me on behalf of the land, that I should not destroy it; but I found no one" (Eze. 22:30).

New Testament typologies of redemptive leadership

Jesus Christ. Much could be written concerning leadership principles and style from the words and example of Jesus Christ. However, there are two key Bible passages that I believe convey the heart of the message on leadership that Jesus wanted to portray to His disciples—shepherd concepts of leadership (John 10) and servant concepts of leadership (Matt. 20).

Shepherd leadership (John 10:1-18). In New Testament times the job responsibility of a shepherd was a position of significance to the economy. In Palestine agriculture and tending flocks of animals were the main occupations. The dryness of the ground made it necessary for the flocks of sheep and cattle to move about during the rainless summer, staying for months at a time in isolated areas far from the dwelling of the owner. This made herding sheep an independent and responsible job. Sometimes the owner or his family did the job, but usually it was done by a hired shepherd.[5]

It was this background of shepherds caring for their flock of sheep that originated the analogy of the pastor (the shepherd) being the overseer of the church members (the flock). This analogy also provides other significant insights for Christian leaders in the church.

In verses 3, 4 we learn that leaders must personally know those they are leading—whether these people be volunteers, employees, or small-group members—in order to understand how best to meet their needs. This is seen in the fact that good shepherds know their sheep by name and calls them, and they follow. This becomes more significant when we understand the New Testament background of being a shepherd. It was normal in Palestine for several flocks of sheep to be kept in a common corral at evening. In the morning, each shepherd would separate their flock from the others by calling to them. In order for the sheep to follow their shepherd, they needed to be connected by trust and respect. The shepherd-leader had to be recognized as a leader, or the sheep would not follow. The principle is clear. As small-group leaders we should seek to become more than just a once-a-week acquaintance with our group members—we should desire to be a true friend.

Servant leadership (Matt. 20). Without Christ being the center of the life, true servant leadership will not be practiced to its fullest degree. The natural human tendency is to lord it over one another, to vie for the top positions. Jesus aptly discusses and analyzes this human tendency in Matthew 20:20-28. Let's take a closer look at verses 20, 21. "Then the mother of Zebedee's sons came to Him with her sons, kneeling down and asking something from Him. And He said to her, 'What do you wish?' She said to Him, 'Grant that these two sons of mine may sit, one on Your right hand and the other on the left, in Your kingdom.' "

The mother of James and John, probably after a discussion with them, demonstrates, along with her sons, the opposite of the principle of being a servant. "Jesus," she pleads, "please give my sons the top two positions in Your kingdom. Let them sit on Your right and left. Will You do this for me?"

In amazement the other 10 disciples listen to this request. Immediately their human nature and lack of "servant leadership" jumps into play. They are angry and indignant! (see verse 24).

Jesus immediately sizes up the situation and sits the three—Mom, James, and John—down for a little talk. " 'You do not know what you ask,' He begins. 'Are you able to drink the cup that I am about to drink, and be baptized with the baptism that I am baptized with?' They said to Him, 'We are able.' So He said to them, 'You will indeed drink My cup, and be baptized with the baptism that I am baptized with; but to sit on My right hand and on My left is not Mine to give, but it is for those for whom it is prepared by My Father' " (verses 22, 23).

Jesus recognized the need to discuss what it truly means to be a leader. The disciples were approaching leadership, position, and power from a secular definition. So Jesus called the other 10 disciples to join James and John and their mother. He then shared these words: "You know that the rulers of the Gentiles lord it over them, and those who are great exercise authority over them. Yet it shall not be so among you; but whoever desires to become great among you, let him be your servant. And whoever desires to be first among you, let him be your slave—just as the Son of Man did not come to be served, but to serve, and to give His life a ransom for many" (verses 25-28).

Ouch! Strong words, but necessary words for Christian leaders—and we are all leaders to someone! A key phrase is Jesus saying that lording it over others through one's authority "shall not be so" among the disciples. *Servant leaders possess authority not because of their position, but because of their attitude toward others.*

When Jesus said the "Son of Man did not come to be served, but to serve" (Matt. 20:28), He was sharing the nucleus of leadership—influencing others to desire to be remade in the image of God. May God empower each leader—including small-group leaders—to fulfill this role!

Slow down and prepare to lead

When I was a boy, I would ride into town with Grandpa in his pickup. The back was strewn with hay from the field or maybe a greasy tractor part that needed to be replaced from the local parts house. It was amazing to me that everyone seemed to know Grandpa. We would stop in the middle of the road, and Grandpa would talk with the passing farmer about cows or alfalfa or laugh at some story from times past. Or we would stop at the roadside café to catch up on local news from the men perched on stools lining the counter.

Somehow, life today seems to have shifted into high gear—at least where I live. Families live on the same street, yet may know personally only the people next door. Life is busy. In order to lead a small group as a shepherd/servant leader, slow down, take a deep breath, and make your group members more than acquaintances, friends that you spend time with. Always remember, a biblical-based leader will "know" and "serve" their small-group members.

---

[1]Data and resources for this chapter can be found in Chapter 1, "Theology, Principles, and Theory of Leadership and Church Growth," of Kurt Johnson, *The Effect of Leadership Behavior and Characteristics on Church Growth for Seventh-day Adventist Churches* (Ph.D. diss., Fuller Theological Seminary, Pasadena, California, 1989).

[2]Henry and Richard Blackaby, *Spiritual Leadership*, pp. 16, 17.

[3]John C. Maxwell, *Developing the Leader Within You*, pp. 1-4.

[4]Robert K. Greenleaf, *Servant Leadership*, p. 10.

[5]Kurt Johnson, *The Effect of Leadership Behavior and Characteristics on Church Growth for Seventh-day Adventist Churches*, pp. 28, 29.

Chapter 12

A SMALL-GROUP LEADER'S JOB DESCRIPTION

I was 18 years old when I led my first "adult" group discussion. I had led out in small-group discussions with my peers, but not with adults I had never met. There I stood, in a little church in Cle Elum, Washington. There were only a handful of us gathered. My grandma had enlisted her budding-preacher grandson to teach the Bible study class for the day. I had carefully prepared my lesson, listing numerous discussion questions—at least I *thought* the questions would lead to lengthy discussions. But I was soon to learn that my group members—composed mostly of gray-haired women like my grandma—would respond with only succinct answers. I wasn't sure how to get a lively discussion going. So 20 minutes later I declared the "discussion" over. To my embarrassment, one dear saint responded, "That's the shortest Sabbath school lesson we've ever had around here."

That experience left me determined to figure out how to lead a discussion if it was the last thing I ever did!

Leading a discussion is one of the key functions of a small-group leader. However, there are numerous other qualities that a group leader needs and will find helpful. We'll take a look at these, but first, let's review once more the small-group leadership team's job descriptions from an earlier chapter.

Group leader

The small-group leader is the person appointed and recognized to serve the group by facilitating and enabling it to achieve its purposes and goals. The group leader's role is essential to the success of the group. The leader needs to be a facilitator of group discussion and personal relationships more than they need to be an authority or distributor of information.

A Bible study group is not the place for a lecture presentation. Rather, it should take the form of a carefully guided discussion. Because the study focuses on Scripture, the leader will need to provide some direction. However, each group member's personal contribution serves as an opportunity for the leader to emphasize the scriptural meaning of the passage being studied.

If you are just beginning as a small-group *leader*, here are some suggestions to get you started:

- Attend a leadership training workshop, read a book like this one, and if possible, participate in a small group as an assistant leader or participant prior to taking on the responsibility of being a small-group leader.
- Facilitate the weekly group meeting.
- Oversee all details of group life in and outside of the weekly meeting.
- Model and encourage participation, sharing, acceptance, and understanding among the members.
- Guide the group in developing a group agreement (or covenant), and goals, and in carrying out the goals that are set.
- Check on members who are absent from the meeting in order to encourage them, meet their needs, and to be aware of any difficulties in their lives.
- Talk and pray weekly about the group with the assistant leader and with the host.
- Seek assistance as needed to ensure positive group life.
- Attend regular scheduled leaders' meetings.

The *assistant leader* should:

- support and encourage the leader through prayer and other means.
- facilitate the group meeting when the leader is absent.
- assist in recruiting new members and following up absent members.
- assist with details such as child-care arrangements, completing and turning in required report forms, and other details as needed.
- attend regularly scheduled leaders' meetings.
- be an apprentice in training (if so desired) to lead a group of their own in the future.

The *host* should:

- provide a comfortable home or location for the meeting.
- arrange seating in the meeting room, adjust the temperature as needed, oversee refreshments if the group has them, and make sure extra Bibles, paper, study guides, pencils, etc., are available.
- answer the door and welcome the members as they arrive.
- make sure the members' needs are met—directing them to the location of the bathroom, telephone, drinking glasses, etc.
- take care of any distractions that may occur during the group meeting, such as the doorbell, telephone, children, pets, etc.

These three positions are important to the success of a small group. However, spiritual preparation is the first and most important step. Through the power of the Holy Spirit, the least-experienced individual can be dramatically effective. The spiritual success of the group is dependent, not so much upon the talents or abilities of the leaders, as upon their willingness to yield themselves to the will and power of God.

Be Responsible

The above job descriptions and list of responsibilities become meaningful only when the leadership team is responsible. I just finished listening to a recent *Voice of Prophecy* radio broadcast. Speaker Mike Tucker's opening illustration involved an employee who is extremely responsible. Pastor Mike can assign Ruth a task and then forget about it. Experience has demonstrated that once she is assigned something to do, consider it done! Ruth will see it to completion no matter what!

Responsibility is paramount for a successful small-group meeting. The leaders have only each other in order to accomplish the task. If they don't do the needed tasks, these things simply will not be done. I was talking recently to the leader of a house church/small group in Orlando, Florida. I asked him what was the most significant lesson he had learned since becoming a group leader. He responded, "Before becoming a group leader in this church plant, I was an elder in my local church. If I did not have time to do a task, I asked someone to do it for me or let the pastor figure it out. In my new leadership role, I have to be responsible or the group will die—fall apart. I am the 'buck stops here' guy. There is no one else. It is me. If I am not responsible to God and to the group He has called me to lead, then I let God down, and some people may not know Jesus Christ because I shirked my duty." Then he added, "That is heavy stuff, huh?" The look on his face told me that his calling as a leader was not something he took lightly.

I read about a psychologist who visited a prison where he interviewed a number of inmates. "Why are you here?" he asked each person. The responses were "I was framed." "Mistaken identity." "I was in the wrong place at the wrong time." "I did not do anything wrong." As the psychologist was leaving the prison, he remarked that he didn't think it was possible to find a larger group of "innocent" people than in this prison.[1] Responsibility was not high on the inmates' list of priorities. However, responsibility is an essential quality for the leaders of a small group.

> I am only one,
> But still I am one.
> I cannot do everything;
> But still I can do something;
> And because I cannot do everything,
> I will not refuse to do the
> Something that I can do.[2]

Leadership guidelines for the group leader and the leadership team[3]

Prayer and spiritual preparation are the primary and most important steps for a group leader. Through the power of the Holy Spirit the least-experienced individual can be dramatically effective. *Your ability to minister is based upon your own spiritual well-being.* As you begin to plan and work toward your small-group meeting, consider doing the following:

1. Set aside time each day for God—Bible study, prayer, and meditation.
2. Spend some of the time praying for your own relationship with God; a good response from the community; support from your local church; your

teaching abilities to be Spirit-filled; your group members; your small-group leadership team; that there will be decisions for Christ and baptisms; and an outpouring of the Holy Spirit in latter-rain proportions. Then wait and listen quietly for God to speak to your heart.

3. Be enthusiastic about studying the Bible—not only to learn and better understand doctrine and theology, but to apply what you learn to daily living. Look for God's promises of strength, faith, power, and soul winning. Write the promises on cards to read or memorize.

4. Study to understand the Scripture passage that will be discussed in the upcoming Bible study. Prayer and Bible study are essential to your understanding and preparation. Don't get sidetracked from this priority. For your own spiritual growth, and to aid your study of a given passage, include Ellen White's books and writings in your reading.

As a group leader you are busy, so make sure you recruit your team members to assist you. Enlist your assistant leader, host, and other members to assist in the following ways:

1. Be excited about your group's discoveries in Scripture. This will encourage the members to deeper study. Even if the ideas are not new to you, it's exciting to watch the group members grow.

2. As your group studies, your personal testimony or experience—or that of a fellow group member—can be helpful to others.

3. Answer questions and provide necessary resource materials. Make sure that the group members are visited as needed and that those who make decisions for Jesus Christ are led into a relationship with Him.

4. Assist those who want to study more deeply into doctrines and encourage them to become church members.

5. Always make sure that the overall needs of the group are being met.

6. Have empathy with the group members. Try to walk in their shoes for a day. Be genuinely interested in showing love and friendliness.

7. Giving personal, individual attention to group members outside of the group meeting can greatly help to meet their personal needs and support them in their personal and spiritual life.

8. A good sense of humor is essential. Everyone loves a good laugh, as long as it is appropriate and timely. Relax! Have fun with your group members.

Caution

As you develop your skills as a leader, it is easy to become discouraged. It is easy to become discouraged if members don't return. It's easy to consider yourself a failure if you experience what you consider to be a poor group study. You will tend to compare yourself and your group unfavorably to other groups and leaders. God gives us good counsel regarding comparing ourselves to others: "For we dare not class ourselves or compare ourselves with those who commend themselves. But they, measuring themselves by themselves, and comparing themselves among themselves, are not wise" (2 Cor. 10:12).

Remember, each person is unique. God made you the way you are, and He has a special place for you. When you compare yourself with others, you are denying God's special creation of your uniqueness. This does not mean you can't learn from your mistakes and the obstacles that come your way—use them as stepping-stones to improvement!

Satan wants you to fail, but God has overcome the evil one! Persevere in faith and prayer, and victory will be yours! God says, "Do not be afraid, but speak, and do not keep silent; for I am with you" (Acts 18:9, 10). This promise is meant for you!

Taking inventory

Because leaders often neglect reviewing their group experiences, they miss opportunities for improvement. Once you have a few group meetings under your belt, evaluate your ability to lead and the quality of your group's experience. Here are a few categories and questions for you as you take inventory.

Planning and preparation:

- Do you adequately prepare? If not, what is needed?
- Do you closely follow your plan? Why or why not? Veering from your plan is not always detrimental, and even sometimes necessary. Be fair to yourself.
- What have you learned that you could include in future planning?

Your leadership techniques:

- Do you lead, or are you led?
- Do you listen, or are you always talking?

- Are you sensitive to the group members' needs?
- Has the group gone off on any tangents from the topic? If so, how did this occur? How could you have handled the situation better? How might you have avoided the situation?

Biblical content:

- Do you ask enough quality questions so that group members can discover, understand, and apply biblical truth?
- Do you keep to the subject of the session?

Group participation:

- Did all the group members come to the session? If not, why not?
- Does your leadership stimulate everyone to contribute his or her best? If not, what could you do to accomplish this?
- Do group members question and talk with each other, rather than just with you?

Personal relationships within the group:

- How well do the members know each other?
- How well do the members listen to each other?

The leader's number one helper—the Holy Spirit

I am reminded of the apostle's experience recorded in Acts 2:1-4. The Bible states that when the tongues of fire rested upon them, "they were all filled with the Holy Spirit and began to speak with other tongues, as the Spirit gave them utterance" (verse 4). For witnessing purposes, God gave them the instant ability to speak in the various languages of the people! However, some were confused about what was taking place. So Peter explained to them what was occurring. "Men of Judea and all who dwell in Jerusalem, let this be known to you, and heed my words. For these men are not drunk, as you suppose, since it is only the third hour of the day. But this is what was spoken by the prophet Joel: 'And it shall come to pass in the last days, says God, that I will pour out of My Spirit on all flesh; your sons and your daughters shall prophesy, your young men shall see visions, your old men shall dream dreams. And on My menservants and on My maidservants I will pour out My Spirit in those days; and they shall prophesy. I will show wonders in heaven above and signs in the earth beneath: blood and fire and vapor of smoke. The sun shall be turned into darkness, and the moon into blood, before the coming of the great and awesome day of the Lord. And it shall come to pass that whoever calls on the name of the Lord shall be saved" (Acts 2:14-21).

Ellen White, reflecting on this promise and experience, made the following comment: "We should pray as earnestly for the descent of the Holy Spirit as the disciples prayed on the Day of Pentecost. If they needed it at that time, we need it more today. All manner of false doctrines, heresies, and deceptions are misleading the minds of men; and without the Spirit's aid, our efforts to present divine truth will be in vain. We are living in the time of the Holy Spirit's power. It is seeking to diffuse itself through the agency of humanity, thus increasing its influence in the world. For if any man drinks of the water of life, it will be in him 'a well of water springing up into everlasting life'; and the blessing will not be confined to himself, but will be shared by others."[4]

Yes, God desires each of us to be Spirit-empowered men and women! Pray for the Spirit; desire to be filled by the Spirit; claim the promise of the infilling of the Spirit; and you will receive *power!* God has promised—and His word is sure.

---

[1] See John C. Maxwell, *Developing the Leader Within You,* p. 170.

[2] Edward Everett Hale, in Jeanie Ashley Bates Greenough, *A Year of Beautiful Thoughts,* June 11.

[3] See The Navigators, *Twelve Steps to Leading Better Bible Studies,* adapted and revised by Garrie F. Williams, pp. 7, 8.

[4] Ellen G. White, in *Review and Herald,* Aug. 25, 1896.

Chapter 13

DEVELOPING SMALL-GROUP LEADERS

A number of years ago I was part of an organization in which the leader included all of the department heads in the decision-making process. One day our board chair was talking to me about an item that was on the agenda of an upcoming executive board meeting. "What do you think should happen with this item?" he asked. My response was to defer to the judgment of our team leader. The board chair responded by saying, "You might as well answer, because your team leader always asks me to give him a day to respond, because he wants to discuss any item with his departmental leaders. Whatever the consensus is will be his answer."

Our team leader's goal was to surround himself with competent staff and then allow them to collectively and cohesively develop a strategy and establish goals for the organization. Our leader had learned that the success of an organization lies in its leadership team. If a leader believes that their role is to acquire more followers who will simply do what the leader says, then the organization will not grow exponentially. However, if a leader believes their role is to develop leaders, then the sky is the limit.

It is said of John Wooden, the UCLA basketball coach who brought the team 10 national championships in a span of 12 years, that his success was the result of his unyielding dedication to the concept of teamwork. He viewed each member of his team as a leader, and he saw his role as developing their leadership skills into a cohesive oneness with the other members of the team.

John Wooden's philosophy was simple: (1) appreciate team members for who they are; (2) believe they will do their very best; (3) praise their accomplishments; and (4) accept your personal responsibility to them as their leader.

True success comes by acquiring good people and keeping them. An organization cannot increase its productivity, but people can. Now, don't get me wrong. Organization is an essential, necessary element, but if you have the wrong people plugged into the slots of your organization, it simply "ain't going to work." This is why selecting and developing leaders is key to your success as a small-group leader.[1]

Pastors often ask me why the small-group ministry in their local church does not grow as they think it should or why it does not match the experience of the churches that are out there teaching the seminars on how to grow small groups in churches just like their church. The greatest success principle I have learned over 35 years of being involved with small groups is this: Just like every area of church life, a local church's small-group success will be no better than its success in developing leaders.

Developing leadership can, and does, occur in the monthly small-group leaders' meeting, but this is not enough. Leadership development involves more than a monthly meeting. Leadership building (a better term, I believe, is "mentoring") involves a daily commitment. If a local church has the goal of developing a growing, vibrant small-group ministry, then, in many cases, it must change its philosophy. It must change the focus from growing followers who are involved in small-group ministry to a focus on developing leaders who become the catalyst of a movement. We must develop leaders who train other leaders.

Remember the example of Moses and Jethro referred to in an earlier chapter? Jethro pointed out to Moses the need to choose and develop leaders whom he could trust to carry out the work. In my ministry I attempt to surround myself with people who are better leaders than I am and who can accomplish tasks that I don't have the skills to do. The better equipped my team leaders become, the stronger our ministry becomes. It is the same with your small-group ministry.

How we learn

You will have to attend one of my training seminars to hear the full story, but I will share enough to whet your interest. When I was a boy, I loved to go fishing. My dad was an avid fisherman and instilled the desire in me. I remember my entire family—two sisters, my brother, my mom, and my dad—all sitting on the bank of the slough near Burbank, Washington, catching bullheads. It always amazed me how long the bullheads could live outside of the water.

Bullheads were easy to catch. A bobber and a worm floating 15 feet from shore would do the trick. As far back as I can remember, I fished. I still have the rod and reel I received for my twelfth birthday—and don't call it an antique; I'm not quite that old yet!

My dad had me watch him tie a swivel on a line and attach a hook to it. He showed me how to hook a bobber on the line and cast it out. When I made my first attempt to cast my line, and my bobber flew off the line, I looked up, waiting for him to reprimand me. Dad was frowning slightly and said, "Next time, be more careful; bobbers cost money!" Because there were four kids to clothe and feed, money was a tight commodity at my house. I was elated when the bobber washed in to shore, and I excitedly retrieved it and saw the smile on Dad's face.

The day that will go down on the first page in the fishing annals of Kurt's fishing history occurred when I was 7 years old. I was fishing with Dad and my uncle along the Snake River when I hooked a bass that put up quite a battle. My uncle hollered for my dad to help me, but Dad simply watched and responded, "He has to learn to fish sometime; leave him alone."

Eventually I brought the fish to shore. I have the photo to prove it, along with a picture of its twin, which I caught 20 minutes later. I learned valuable lessons from my dad about teaching someone to acquire a skill or technique. It is a simple four-step procedure:

Step 1:   I watched Dad fish.
Step 2:   Dad taught me how to fish.
Step 3:   Dad watched me do what he taught me. He made suggestions.
Step 4:   I taught my kids how to fish, based on what my dad taught me.

When I was pastoring churches, I conducted ongoing training classes in which I taught my members how to give a Bible study, make a home visit, lead a small group, etc. These classes were successful, because I took the time to follow the steps listed above. For the past 26 years I have ministered as a trainer/consultant with church pastors and members to equip members for ministry. My greatest frustration has come from the fact that in many churches equipping usually follows this pattern.

Step 1: A member wants to learn how to fish (start a small group).

Step 2: An afternoon or weekend seminar on how to fish (lead a small group) is conducted.

Step 3: The fishing instructor (sometimes me) encourages the members to go fishing (start small groups), and then the instructor goes home. Instructors are sometimes available later for follow-up consultation, but they depend on the local leaders to do most of the hands-on training.

Step 4: Some members try fishing on their own (starting a small group). Their line gets tangled up; they lose their bait; and they quit fishing in frustration.

Fortunately, sometimes a pastor (or an experienced member in the congregation) takes those who want to be fishers (small-group members/leader) and helps them apply what they have learned in the previous three steps—or at least an adapted version of these steps.

Three learning components

In order for equipping to be successful, it must not leave out any of the three learning components that are included in the above steps. All three learning components are vital to lifestyle change or successful equipping. These learning components are:

1. Cognitive learning. This component involves sharing information or knowledge verbally or in written form. Usually this occurs through reading books, attending seminars, watching DVDs, or listening to CDs. This is a vital step, because gathering information usually enables someone to gain an overview of the topic. The negative side to cognitive learning is that it can cause an information overload if too much material is shared without an accompanying hands-on experience with each concept shared.

2. Application learning. Application learning is learning through action. The person participates in the activity, rather than merely reading or hearing about it. For example, I may teach you verbally how to visit a group member and demonstrate the process to you. But if I then take you with me on a visit and you are involved in a real-life visit, I have just taken you to a new level of learning. The cognitive information is now more valuable to you, because you have seen it applied in a positive manner.

3. Transformational learning. This type of learning involves lifestyle or behavioral change. The information learned verbally and practiced in a realistic situation now becomes part of one's lifestyle through transformational learning. In order for someone to move effectively to this step there must be (a) ongoing application learning, (b) ongoing commitment on the part of the church members, and (c) a mentor to function as an encourager and skills trainer.

Most churches and parachurch organizations are really good at providing cognitive support, but they are often weak on application learning and weaker yet on making sure that transformational learning takes place.

Sometimes a local church asks me to come and teach a seminar on how to visit Bible study interests. In order to apply these three steps of learning I ask for the following to take place in preparation for my arrival:

1. I ask the pastor to select two church members who have had some experience in door-to-door visitation and who have the ability to show someone else how to visit.

2. I set up visitation appointments for a Friday—at 10:00 a.m. with the pastor and at 1:00 p.m. with the pastor and the two selected church members.

3. At 10:00 a.m. I take the pastor with me and let him watch me make a visit. Then I watch the pastor make a visit. Afterward we talk about these visits together.

4. At 1:00 p.m. I take one of the church members with me, and the pastor takes the other member with him. The members watch us make a visit. Then the pastor and I let the members lead out in a visit.

5. On Sabbath afternoon I conduct the seminar. During the seminar I talk about how to make a visit. I demonstrate how to make a visit. I have the seminar participants role-play visits with each other. I have the pastor and the two church members who went visiting on Friday talk about their experiences.

6. Next, I set up appointments for the seminar attendees to go visiting with the pastor and the two members who visited on Friday. If my schedule permits, I stay and help with the actual visitation.

7. The pastor and the two members continue the process of training, feedback, and mentoring of those involved in visitation.

8. I am available for consultation, and sometimes I follow up with additional seminars and hands-on assistance.

Is this process perfect? No. Does it work? Yes. But it still has its pitfalls. Experience has shown me that nothing we do will be 100 percent effective, but if we do not aim for the bull's-eye, I guarantee we will not hit it. It takes a commitment of time and ongoing hands-on involvement to develop successful visitation teams. This same pattern can be applied to developing small-group leaders or to any other area of training. The bottom line is that we cannot equip others for ministry as we usually try to do it—holding a training event for six to eight weeks and then moving on to some other project. *Developing and equipping leaders is a long-term process—not an event.*

I have another suggestion to get more people involved in small-group ministry, but first let's discuss a traditional, and somewhat successful, way of equipping small-group leaders. If you use this method, it will work.

Equipping small-group leaders

Remember, the ultimate purpose of a small group is to lead group members into a saving relationship with Jesus Christ and to become fully devoted disciples. This does not eliminate the foundational elements of unconditional friendship, acceptance, and love. However, the Christian's ultimate job description involves bringing people to Jesus. Keeping this in mind helps us realize that it is essential to develop small-group leaders to lead their own groups! If each equipper/mentor trained two people a year, and those two trained two more people, and so on, the sheer multiplication of leaders would also multiply ministry and the salvation of many.

If you are a local pastor or the coordinator of small groups in your local church, then recruiting small-group leaders and developing new leaders (apprentice leaders) is a large part of your responsibility. Let's take a look together at managing this part of your ministry responsibility.

Selecting small-group leaders

Every member of a local church and every member of a small group is a potential leader. But you cannot mentor all of them to become small-group leaders. You should always lead and nurture everyone within your realm of ministry contact, but you should carefully select those who will become small-group leaders.

Caution: None of us possesses all of the qualities of Christian leadership, especially in the area of spiritual growth. As you consider being a small-group leader, the question to ask yourself is: Do I desire to grow daily to be like Jesus and do I have a desire to develop my competence and skills as a group leader? If your answer is yes, then you are almost there!

Whom should you choose for a small-group leader?

* The one assigned to look for new leaders should first *pray* for leaders. And those who feel called to be a small-group leader should *pray* for God's leading in their life and ministry.
* Choose individuals who have embraced the vision and need for small groups. Look for those who believe in the philosophy and value of the plan for small-group ministry in your local church.
* Choose people in whom you have confidence and in whom you believe—those whose potential you see and who know you believe in their potential. This way, both of you are committed to the development process.
* Look for people who enjoy being a shepherd, who build relationships easily, who have a heart for people, and who have a desire to be involved in small groups. Some who are excellent leaders in other capacities do not make good small-group leaders, because they lack the necessary temperament and relational skills. Sometimes the only way to know how a person will do as a small-group leader is to allow them to become an assistant leader and give the individual opportunities to lead the group.
* Look for people who have been part of a small group and who enjoy the experience and feel a calling to be part of a small-group leadership team.
* Observe people in the group or other areas of ministry who seem to possess the characteristics of a small-group leader.

When you have chosen potential leaders (apprentice leaders), what is the next step?

- Determine what each individual needs personally in order to develop into a small-group leader. Each person is different. That is why you cannot have everyone follow the same equipping track. Some foundational elements of developing leaders are applicable to everyone, but every person being mentored must receive personalized assistance.
- Give continued feedback. This is critical early in the training process. Always be open, fair, kind, and objective.
- Be available. This means making one-on-one time. Availability means time. It means interruptions. It means frustration. It means excitement and joy. However, the time spent will result in a strong leader who can eventually help develop other leaders. Several members of my staff will periodically call me on the phone or want to visit with me in the office. Often our discussions have nothing to do with their work, but with life development issues. These discussions take time, but for me, they are not interruptions; they are time well spent in developing stronger leaders for Jesus Christ.

Recently I had an appointment with a podiatrist to obtain new orthotics for my shoes. New York Yankee memorabilia covered the walls of the diagnosis room. The doctor was a Yankee fan. I was sympathetic; I still have my Mickey Mantle and Roger Maris baseball cards I got from cereal boxes when I was a kid. I noticed one picture in particular on his wall—a photo of the entire 1977 Yankee World Series championship team, including the coaches and trainers. As I looked at the photo, I was struck by the thought that the world's best baseball players still needed coaches to help them be the best that they could be. You would think that players could just play and win once they made it to the major leagues, but that is not the case.

Think of what goes into a winning team. Just to name a few items: equipment (gloves, balls, bats, etc.), uniforms, exercises, weight training, running, treadmills, step climbers, medical care, learning team philosophy, team-building time, pep talks, various coaches, physical therapists, trainers, managers, preseason games, regular season games—and the list goes on and on. There are even team psychologists to prepare the players for dealing with stress or other personal issues that might get in the way of playing to their optimum level.

Those who are attempting to equip/mentor small-group leaders, then, are like athletic coaches. They must provide more than simply a weekend seminar on leading a small group. Equippers must be part of an ongoing process. Equippers/mentors should be those who themselves (1) have led a small group or who are currently small-group leaders; (2) are able to cast the vision for what a small group should accomplish; (3) inspire potential leaders to want to be involved in small-group ministry; (4) make sure the potential leader experiences the joy of seeing lives transformed through a small-group experience; and (5) are available to answer questions, encourage, and support potential leaders through talking together and providing resources such as books, audio CDs, seminar suggestions, etc.

Let's break it down a step further and simplify the task of those who mentor small-group leaders.

1. *Model Christian growth through your own life.* Paul wrote, "Imitate me, just as I also imitate Christ" (1 Cor. 11:1).

2. *Help the small-group leaders you are mentoring to grow in their spiritual walk.* Paul counseled young Timothy, "Preach the word! Be ready in season and out of season. Convince, rebuke, exhort, with all longsuffering and teaching" (2 Tim. 4:2).

3. *Cast a vision for your leaders.* Help them dream about how their group can affect the group members, the community, and the local church. "Hope deferred makes the heart sick, but when desire comes, it is a tree of life" (Prov. 13:12).

4. *Provide training in key small-group skills, so the apprentice leaders can be more effective in meeting the needs of the group members.* "He Himself [Jesus Christ] gave some to be . . . teachers, for the equipping of the saints for the work of ministry, for the edifying of the body of Christ" (Eph. 4:11, 12).[2]

Notice that the first step involves the mentor's own spiritual life. This is the foundation upon which the next three steps build. Never skip any of the steps, and follow them in the order listed. For example, if you go straight to the training component, skipping steps 2 and 3, the potential leader will not succeed. Small-group leadership is a God thing, not a human thing. In addition, as trust develops between the equipper and those being equipped, spending time on each step will strengthen the apprentice small-group leaders.

The role of the apprentice small-group leader

1. Care. Love and support your small-group leader and the group members. Take an active role in sharing this responsibility with your leader. This can include not only your assistance during the group time, but personal contact, by telephone or face-to-face, with members outside of the group.

2. Learn. Learn by observing your small-group leader. Notice what the leader does and does not do. Debrief each meeting, discussing the group process. Look at why the leader said and did certain things and discuss future approaches and solutions. In addition, attend seminars, read books, watch training DVDs, etc.

3. Lead. You need experience. The leader should allow you, as an apprentice, to gain experience by leading out in certain aspects of the meeting—the sharing time, prayer time, or a couple of the discussion questions. As your skills develop, you will eventually be able to lead the entire group experience with the leader present.

4. Look. Apprentice leaders will eventually need to build a team. This means you will need an assistant leader, or apprentice, and a host/hostess. So the apprentice leader should always be on the lookout for individuals who might fill these roles when they have their own group.

Note: Both assistant leaders and apprentice leaders are mentioned in this paragraph. Not all assistant leaders are apprentice leaders. Some assistant leaders do not want to become group leaders, but feel called to be an assistant leader. An apprentice leader is someone preparing to become a small-group leader.[3]

Curriculum for developing small-group leaders

This is an interesting topic because of the varied approaches that exist. Some small-group ministry organizations have an in-depth training curriculum that takes months or a couple of years to complete. Others cite the biblical counsel: "Of making many books there is no end, and much study is wearisome to the flesh" (Eccl. 12:12). They take a more simple approach, believing that we learn better by experience.

I believe in being as simple as possible. If you make it too difficult, people will become discouraged and quit. Others won't even begin! My personal experience indicates that keeping the basic training simple and then individualizing additional assistance as needed is a successful approach. Here are my suggestions.

1. If you are starting from scratch and have no trained leaders in your local church, the pastor or a lay leader with a vision for small groups (with the pastor's support and encouragement) should do one of two things—both, if possible. Attend a small-group training workshop and select several people in your congregation who will be equipped to carry out a small-group ministry.

2. Read books on how to conduct a small-group meeting. (In addition to the book you are reading, another by the same author is *Small Groups for the End Time*.)

3. Watch training DVDs.

4. Locate someone with small-group experience in a neighboring church or by contacting your conference office for a suggestion. Visit with the group leader, attend their small-group meeting, and observe what they do in the meeting.

5. If small groups already exist in your local church, then join one of the groups. Be a group member and learn small-group life. Eventually, become an assistant or apprentice leader with someone to mentor/coach you.

6. Attend your local church monthly small-group leaders' meetings, where you will learn about the joys and struggles of being a small-group leader.

7. Continue to read books on small groups.

8. Most important—pray!

Basic topics to learn about as a small-group leader

1. Biblical foundations of small groups.

2. How to find small-group members.

3. What to do and say on opening night.

4. What to do and say on the second and subsequent nights.

5. Learn how to lead out in the three parts of the small-group agenda—sharing time, Bible study time, and prayer time.

6. Job descriptions of the small-group leader, assistant leader, and host/hostess.

7. How to deal with the various types of personalities in your group—the talkative person, the quiet person, the new Christian, the seeker, etc.

8. Obtaining decisions for Christ.

9. How to decide what curriculum materials to use when you first begin as a small-group leader.

10. Suggestions on developing your own personal devotional life of Bible study and prayer.

11. What to do with group members who are in crisis—depressed, facing marital issues, dealing with spousal abuse, experiencing children/parent conflicts, etc.

12. Child care for your group members.

13. Handling conflict in a small group.

14. Understanding your own leadership style and the difference between facilitating a group and teaching a group.

15. The role of the Holy Spirit in one's personal life, ministry, and small-group experience.

16. Understanding the concept of witnessing and discipleship. Distinguishing between God's role in witnessing and our role.

These are simply a summary of the topics that a small-group leader should be exposed to in order to be an effective small-group leader. Experience has shown that a basic understanding of group life through experience and by reading a book such as this one lays a good foundation for launching a small-group ministry. However, do not wait to research every topic before you begin. Get started and keep learning!

Core teams

Another organizational suggestion that some churches have used to increase the number of small-group leaders and to more effectively involve the entire group in being assistants within the group is to develop "core teams" within each small group.

The concept is simple. Involve every willing group member in the planning and carrying out of the plans for the group meetings. Instead of the group leader, assistant leader, and host/hostess carrying the entire load, invite the group members to colead. The group leader still sets the direction and guides the group meeting, but the others have an opportunity to lead out in the sharing time or prayer time. Or to assist with follow-up with group members or to plan for the children's meeting. In other words, anyone who wants to have a responsibility is given one. The core team members meet together on an agreed-upon regular basis, discuss the list of duties, and volunteer for the responsibilities they would like to assume.

Core teams provide members with a sense of deeper ownership of the group. Also, the process helps others learn how to be a group leader. Out of this mix, more group leaders will emerge simply because more people are involved in leading. In addition, core teams bond the members closer together. Ideas are shared by all in ways that strengthen the group and make it more effective. Everyone involved becomes a shareholder in the group's success, rather than being merely a participant who hopes that the group will meet their needs.[4]

This is why I believe that some house-church models today are attractive to some people. I visited a house church that operates like a small group and follows a core leadership model. Everyone who was willing to assume some responsibility was involved. There were tables to move, floors to clean, prayers to say, Bible studies to participate in, kids to watch and play with, and a number of other duties. When almost everyone in attendance is involved in doing something, there is a tendency for those sitting back and watching to want to jump in and participate. New friendships develop in this environment, and ownership of the group and a sense of belonging emerge very quickly.

Be a leader

Do not be afraid to begin being involved as a small-group leader. If you wait to begin until you think you are ready and have all the answers, you will never start! Begin by simply beginning. Sure, you will make a few mistakes, but you will learn quickly. Experience does that for us. Remember, through the Holy Spirit, God can take what we consider to be a failure and use it for His good.

I learned this lesson as an intern pastor right out of college. I had just finished preaching a sermon and greeting the people at the door. I felt that my sermon that morning was a failure. I walked back into my office and sat down at the desk. The senior pastor came in and said, "That was a good message, Kurt."

"I don't think so," I responded. "My delivery was not my best. My points were not as concise and coherent as they should have been . . ." On and on I went. The pastor was refuting my points and trying to encourage his discouraged intern. At that moment there was a knock on the office door.

A woman I had never met put her head in the door and said to me, "I was really blessed by your sermon today. It was meant for me. How can I get a copy of the message?"

I had written out the sermon fully. I reached into my Bible, pulled out my manuscript, and handed it to her. "Here," I said, "you can have the manuscript."

With a surprised look on her face, she said, "Won't you want it to preach the sermon again?"

"That's OK," I answered. "I probably won't ever preach it again anyway."

Looking surprised and pleased, she thanked me profusely and left. The senior pastor smiled and said, "See, it wasn't that bad after all."

I learned that day to do my best and that God would take my feeble efforts and cover them with His divine power, making something wonderful out of my shortcomings.

So as you begin as a small-group leader, trust God. Get started. It is going to be OK. God is really the small-group leader; you are His apprentice. And guess what—because God never fails, it is impossible for you to fail!

---

[1]John Maxwell, *Developing the Leaders Around You*, pp. 1, 2.
[2]Bill Donahue and Greg Bowman, *Coaching Life-changing Small Group Leaders*, p. 30.
[3]Bill Donahue, *Leading Life-changing Small Groups*, p. 70.
[4]Randall Neighbour, *The Naked Truth About Small Group Ministry*, p. 185.

Chapter 14

WHY SMALL GROUPS ARE STRUGGLING IN SOME CHURCHES

Several years ago I received an invitation to speak at a pastors' retreat on the topic of small groups. The individual inviting me said, "We believe that small groups are an essential part of church life, but none of the churches in our conference has a strong small-group program. I would like you to tell us what the problem is and what we can do to fix it."

The heart of the matter—questions to answer

In order to identify the problem and suggest answers, we must first begin by clarifying our expectations of small groups and then explore the reasons that small groups struggle in some churches.

First, one must decide what the goals are for a small-group ministry in their local church. Is the goal to have everyone involved in a small group that meets weekly, bimonthly, or monthly? Or are small groups simply a desirable option? Does the church want *small groups* to be the heart of the church, or is the heart to be *ministry programs*? Does the church want to continue with ministry programs and still provide a small-group experience for all members? What are small groups expected to accomplish—witnessing, leading unbelievers to Jesus, discipleship, prayer/Bible study, friendship, mentoring, etc.?

I am not suggesting that you call a church board meeting or a business session and discuss these questions. If you do, dissension and division could well be the result, and the church may be thrown into chaos. Experience testifies to this very real possibility. However, the answers to these questions will help determine whether the church's expectations for small groups are being met. So surround yourself with a small group of local church leaders and have a healthy discussion on the topic.

The answer to the questions

You see, the core of the issue revolves around two things—theology, yes, but ultimately around the structure that your church chooses to accomplish its purpose or function. If you asked most pastors to state their goals or desires for their church members, they would answer something like this:

"I want my members to be fully devoted disciples of Jesus Christ. This means that they have a group of close friends who minister to one another, meet one another's needs, and provide support, accountability for each other. When one is sick, the others visit that person. When one needs encouragement, the others provide it. The members pray and study their Bibles in a way that deepens their spirituality and faith. All members understand their uniqueness and ministry gifts and are using those gifts to encourage their fellow Christians and to lead the unchurched to Christ. Members are mentoring/discipling someone else in a relationship with Jesus. Kingdom growth is taking place both spiritually and numerically. The pastor is encouraging, equipping, and supporting the members involved in ministry."

The core of the matter is: What is the best way to organize the church to accomplish these biblical goals?

Related to all of the above questions are the major reasons small groups struggle in some churches. Here, from my perspective, are the top six reasons:

1. *Beginning with the wrong launch strategy.* You started "big" instead of "small."

2. *Following a pastor-dependent model.* In American society today and on some other continents, the current role of the pastor is based on a pastor-dependent model for caregiving and spiritual nurture/growth of the church members.

3. *Failing to note a structural/organizational issue.* (This item arises from point number 2 above.) Because the majority of North American churches, as well as some other world locations, are dependent on the pastor for caregiving and soul winning, church members do not see a need to belong to a

small group. And because most North American churches are organized on a program-based model rather than a small-group model, the small-group experience is not part of the DNA of church life.

4. *Church members are too busy.* Today, both mom and dad work. Add family responsibilities, school, household chores, entertainment, hobbies, etc., and many families do not have room for any "extras." Some members can add a few church meetings or other ministry options, but their time is limited.

5. *In most churches a discipleship/mentor experience is not in place for new Christians, including current members.* Thus, there is little understanding of spiritual gifts and ministry service. And help for those who want to be involved in ministry is often lacking.

6. *Failing to establish a "praying church."* Prayer is a necessity.

Let's now briefly examine each of these six reasons.

Reason 1: Beginning with the wrong launch strategy

Many churches launch small groups with announcements from the pulpit and flyers in the church bulletin and on hallway bulletin boards. Small groups are organized before the launch, and members are encouraged to sign up. Minimal training for group leaders and lack of a regular leaders' meeting leads the "big splash" of the introduction to quickly become a "low sputter." The solution is to start small and increase the number of groups and participants slowly. (See Chapter 6 "Small Groups 201—Understanding Your Group" for suggestions on how to begin small groups.)

Reasons 2 and 3: The pastor-dependent model and structural/organizational issues

I was attending a convention on the topic of sharing one's faith in the marketplace. The speaker had finished his presentation on what he believed to be the key issue affecting the state of the church—which was that Adventists were not following the counsel of Ellen White nor the legacy handed down to them from the church pioneers regarding the role of the pastor and laity. The pastor, he said, was supposed to be an equipper and church planter; he was not to be assigned to one church to take care of it.

The response of some of my friends was "Amen, I agree!" Others said, "This is the twenty-first century, not the nineteenth. The way we equip and organize the church must change with culture and time." Today, for some, this discussion continues.

Some individuals believe that in order for the pastor and church members to fulfill their biblical role, the church must get back to its early church, pre-Constantine model. (Constantine was the Roman emperor when Christianity was declared to be the official religion of the empire.) This early-church model includes, as we have discussed in previous chapters, both house churches and large-group meetings that include an Acts 2:41-47 experience. Furthermore, from an Adventist perspective, our church history illustrates a church-planting, ministry-equipping, small-group model.

In this book's chapter on early church history, documentation is given from A. G. Daniells that at least up through the early part of the twentieth century the Adventist Church did not have "settled pastors."[1]

It appears from Elder Daniells' remarks that ordained ministers were at that time trainer/equippers, church planters, evangelists, and overseers of groups of churches. In his research Russell Burrill shares the following interesting insight on this topic. D. M. Canright, an Adventist minister who had left the denomination and written against it, contended that he had been a prominent minister in the Adventist Church because he pastored 18 churches at one time. The Kalamazoo *Telegraph*, Kalamazoo, Michigan, recorded the church's official response to Canright's statement: "The facts in the case are these: Seventh-day Adventist churches maintain their regular worship without the assistance of any located pastors, leaving our entire ministry free to act as evangelists in new fields. As a consequence, many of our churches pass long periods without any preaching, and consequently conference committees aim to arrange the labor in the state so that ministers will occasionally be at liberty to visit the churches, to help encourage them in the Christian life by a few meetings."[2]

Ellen White reflected similar thoughts about church members needing involvement in ministry as quoted in the same chapter on early church history.[3]

Keep in mind that Elder Daniells' remarks were made 100 years ago. The way we "do church" and the job description of the pastor in the twenty-first century has adapted with societal changes. The pastor is essential to the health and mission of the church. The pastor's value as a leader, equipper, mentor, spiritual nurturer of the body of Christ is foremost in the organization of the church. The point I want us to glean from these historical comments and Ellen White's comments is that the pastor's biblical role must not be sidetracked by "perceived duties" from meaningful church members or other leaders.

Equipping is essential

This philosophy in early Adventism was based upon 1 Corinthians 12:4-7, which speaks of "diversities of gifts," "differences of ministries," but states that "the manifestation of the Spirit is given to each one for the profit of all." The philosophy was also based on the realities of an Adventist Church that was a fledging denomination just getting started. In fact, early on there was quite a discussion over "church organization," with many earnestly opposed to any formal organization or to calling the church a "denomination." The early pioneers saw the Adventist Church as a "movement" or a "mission." Some believed if Adventists called themselves a denomination, they would settle into a "cathedral model" of organization and our member/pastor passion for mission would be lost.

My purpose here is not to debate whether the pre-1912 Adventist pastor's role is the model that the Adventist Church should follow in the twenty-first century. However, I do want to point out that according to the Bible and the writings of Ellen White, *a key role of the pastor is to equip church members for service/ministry*. As we have seen in the preceding chapters, a small-group experience is mandated by Scripture and supported by Ellen White. Thus, equipping for ministry must include small groups for outreach and nurture.

The twenty-first-century Adventist Church and our postmodern society may dictate additional functions for the pastor and a role that is much different than it was in 1912. But if the pastor's function of equipping church members for ministry is buried in a myriad of board meetings, counseling sessions, and administrative duties, then the pastor is not being allowed to fulfill his or her biblical injunction.

The question

So the question becomes: Is it possible to discontinue the current program-based model and shift to another? The answer is yes—if a group of church members makes the decision to do so. However, without persecution of the church, it is doubtful that many would choose to make the change. Persecution would force the church to adjust its program-based model.

But if local church members and pastors are content with their current church model, but want to change the dynamic to more fully capture the essence of Acts 2:41-47, is there a way to do this without creating disaster in the church? I believe the answer is yes. Easy? Not always. But possible. A pastor-dependent model and a program-based model do not mean that small-group ministry cannot flourish in a local church. It simply means that one has to recognize the issues/barriers involved and discover a workable solution.

The role of the church member in ministry

The role of the church member is to be involved in ministry based upon his or her spiritual gifts. This involvement will include caring/ministering for fellow church members and those who are unchurched yet interested in spiritual things. This will free the pastor to equip yet others for ministry, to plant churches, and to organize the churches for ministry.

According to 1 Corinthians 12 and Ephesians 4, this means that organizationally the church is covered. Some are "apostles, some prophets, some evangelists, and some pastors and teachers"—for what?—"for the equipping of the saints for the work of ministry, for the edifying of the body of Christ" (Eph. 4:11, 12). What are the "saints" supposed to do? Be involved in ministry. Timothy said some are elders and deacons to carry out the work of the church (see 1 Tim. 3). And if one studies the topic of spiritual gifts in the Bible and the involvement of men and women in ministry, it is clear that the management/leadership of the local church is dependent upon qualified, Spirit-filled followers of Jesus.

In Ellen White's view, church members are to grow in discipleship simply by being involved in telling others about Jesus. "Those who would be overcomers must be drawn out of themselves; and the only thing which will accomplish this great work, is to become intensely interested in the salvation of others"[4]

Jesus said, "The harvest truly is plentiful, but the laborers are few" (see Matt. 9:37, 38; Luke 10:2). My answer? Some are joyfully involved; others are sitting at home wanting to be involved in telling others about Jesus;

others would be involved if they understood they were supposed to! They have never been instructed regarding the role of a disciple. Many church members simply don't know how to get started or whom to ask. A program-based church model, according to some, makes this involvement more difficult than does the small-group model. The church must be intentional and organize for equipping and service. Let me illustrate.

Program-based Model

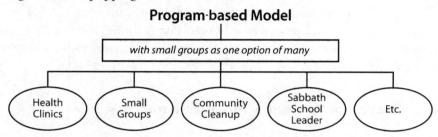

- The majority of North American Adventist churches follow this model.
- Small groups are one of many options.
- All are invited from the "front of the church" to be involved in the programs, but there is sometimes no intentional strategy in place to involve everyone.
- Time, family and work responsibilities, board meetings, etc., limit church member involvement.
- Relational experience is dependent upon the Sabbath school class, usually not weekly small groups for all.

Program-based Model

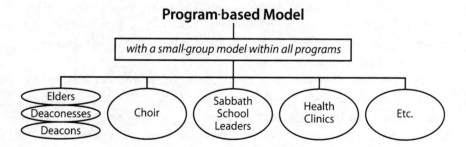

- Every church ministry/program becomes a small group.
- The elders, Sabbath school division leaders, the choir, etc., become a small group.

- Leaders or a team member of each program/ministry/committee are trained/equipped for small-group leadership within the program team.
- Programs/events are reduced in frequency to give members the needed time to add the small-group component.
- The small-group experience for all program/ministry groups includes a designated time for all participants of a given program team to sit in a circle. The agenda includes: sharing, Bible study, prayer, ministry planning/evaluation.

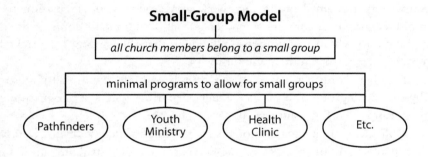

Small-Group Model

| all church members belong to a small group |
| minimal programs to allow for small groups |

Pathfinders · Youth Ministry · Health Clinic · Etc.

- All church members belong to a small group.
- The small group meets weekly, twice a month, or monthly.
- In some cases the weekly small groups meet also as Sabbath school classes.
- Ministry programs are kept to a minimum to give church members time to be involved in the weekly small groups. (Pathfinders, youth program, etc., still function.)
- The small group serves as a team of people ministering to one another and reaching out into the community to the unchurched.
- The weekly worship service includes a small-group experience.
- Small groups take priority over programs; very few programs exist that do not arise from small groups.

Ministry occurs naturally

Anyone who has been involved in a small-group experience knows personally that ministry, community, and bonding naturally take place when a group of people regularly share their life struggles and joys, pray together, search for solutions in the Bible, and reach out to others in the community. When a member of the group is sick, the group members rally around that person and his or her family. They provide food, visit the sick person, and meet other related needs. When this occurs throughout the church family, then the local church has just shifted from a pastor-dependent model to a member-dependent model. This does not mean that the pastor is not aware of illnesses among the members; he may even visit the sick person. But the group is the *primary* support system.

In addition, if the program/ministry teams are reaching out into the community, the small-group members know each member's passion for ministry. They pray for each member and also attempt to connect them to people to whom to minister—individuals that their group has reached through its ministry in the community.

In other words, a program-based church with an intentional philosophy that small groups must be the experience from which all of church life flows, can have a flourishing small-group church.

Will this church organizational structure look different than the early church of the book of Acts or the Adventist Church structure in A. G. Daniells' day? Yes, but the biblical principles that undergirded those early beginnings will be present. It goes back to the principle of "new wine in old wineskins." The wine is the same; it is the container that is different.

Small-group church

I have a pastor friend who has experienced, to some degree, both of the previously described church models. The experience has led him to develop a small-group house church. I visited his house church. The experience went like this: We met together at 10:30 a.m. for a light breakfast. The children met with the adults for the first 15 minutes. We sang songs together, and everyone shared what they had done that week to help someone or to simplify their life to make room for God.

After the sharing time, the children went into a bedroom for a children's program (Sabbath school). The adults studied a prepared Bible study led by a lay member. At the end of the Bible study time, we stood together in a circle and prayed for each other and for the group members who were not able to attend. A chair was placed in the middle of the circle, and the group prayed for God to bring someone to fill the chair the next week—the members are encouraged to invite a friend.

Then the children rejoined the adults for lunch. Everyone helped prepare lunch, talking together and becoming better acquainted. Some shared their struggles. Two women were struggling to quit smoking and were looking forward to baptism. Another was looking for a job. Someone else was contemplating moving to another state for work and to be near her spouse's family. Fellowship, support, and love abounded. About 2:00 p.m. the cleanup was done, and everyone headed home.

The concept behind small-group church is to have numerous small-group house churches in a given city. These would meet together on some regular basis for a large-group meeting that would include worship and fellowship. In this scenario, the pastor's role is to organize the groups, train members to minister, and to lead house churches.

Reality of church life

My ministry has provided me with the unique and blessed opportunity to travel around the world and worship with many people. I have discovered that very few cultures worship and conduct ministry exactly the same. There is diversity and various preferences in how to carry out the directives and principles of Scripture regarding worship, discipleship, soul winning, and meeting the needs of church members and the community. I know committed Christians who prefer the program-based model, others who prefer the small-group model, and still others who like the blended model. However, we must make sure that we have a "two-winged church," as one author describes it—a balance, with both a small-group and a large-group experience.

Another reality of church life is that some people, based on their personality, do not like a small group. They do not like the experience. Some small-group proponents would say that this is precisely why such individuals *should* attend a small group—"they simply don't know yet that the small-group experience would transform them. Whether they know it or not, they need a small-group church or cell-church experience." I would agree that everyone needs the Acts 2:41-47 experience, but unless it is provided in an alternate format, you will most likely never get everyone involved.

(See Chapter 5, "Small Groups 101—The Basics," particularly the section describing the various types of groups.) I have had people tell me that they receive their Acts 2 experience through their circle of two or three friends with whom they intentionally interact, and that they are involved in an outreach project. Thus they have a small-group experience without an organized small group.

A final thought

As you contemplate which model you prefer, the key factor is that your model of choice includes a small-group experience for everyone. As long as your church follows the biblical injunction discussed in this book—making sure that the biblical principles regarding discipleship, witnessing, ministry, evangelism, and Christ-centered community are being applied and lived out in church life—I do not think God is particular about which model you follow.

The bottom line is that the Bible and the Spirit of Prophecy show that church life includes ministry taking place both "house to house" and in "the temple." In the early Christian church there was both small-group time and large-group time. The purpose being to equip the church to work for the church members and unbelievers. How you structure church life in your particular situation and culture to accomplish this task is a choice that God will show you through Bible study, prayer, and the guidance of the Holy Spirit.

I am reminded of the disciples saying to Jesus, "'We saw someone who does not follow us casting out demons in Your name, and we forbade him because he does not follow us.' But Jesus said, 'Do not forbid him. . . . For he who is not against us is on our side'" (Mark 9:38-40).

One must be extremely careful they do not choose the easy way out and use culture and time as an excuse not to change the status quo that may need changing. God calls us to faithfulness and honesty with His Word and ministry calling.

Reason 4: Church members are too busy

A number of years ago I spent several weeks in a rural village with no electricity (except for a generator), cell phone, or clock to run my life by. Daily I taught a field school and conducted an evangelistic reaping meeting.

I was blessed! To be honest, it was one of the best experiences of my life! I loved the simple pace of life and being disconnected from all of the gadgets that normally rule my day.

Life is busy! In an earlier chapter we discussed the evolving role of the working mother and what this means today in terms of volunteerism and ministry. Between work, commuting to and from work, family responsibilities, shuttling kids to soccer or football practice, school, church outings and programs, church board meetings, trying to get a break by watching a favorite television program, keeping up with Facebook and Twitter, having an exercise program, family time, etc., it's tough to squeeze in time for being part of a small group.

Something has to give if members are going to find time for a small-group experience. Church leadership needs to help members reflect on their lifestyle and involvement in church life as well as on the leaders' expectations for members. Even if a church had no small groups, members juggling all the activities outlined above would not have time for any church extras outside of Sabbath morning.

Reason 5: A discipleship/mentor experience is not in place for new Christians, including current members.

As a result, there is need for a deeper understanding of spiritual gifts, ministry service, or how to assist others to be involved in ministry. In order for church members to develop a life-changing habit of prayer and Bible study, to become involved in ministry, to lead others to accept Jesus, and to mentor them in their journey, church leadership must first disciple the existing members. When this is accomplished, small groups will have an opportunity to flourish.

Reason 6: Failing to establish a "praying church."

Several years ago a friend of mine came up with an excellent idea. His idea was that active, attending church members want to see their neighbors have an opportunity to accept Jesus and to live a fulfilled life. But because Christians are busy and sometimes fearful about sharing their faith, he needed to develop a plan to make sharing simple. Here is his plan:

1. Each member was to accept a group of 10 to 20 homes in their neigh-
    borhood as a personal mission field.
2. During the member's daily worship, when they drove or walked by
    these designated homes, they were to pray for the families that lived
    there—that God would meet their needs and that they would accept
    Jesus into their lives.
3. If the member chose to become further involved (and this was optional),
    there were suggestions and help for becoming friends with these fami-
    lies through personal contact, with the eventual goal of inviting them
    to be part of a personal or small-group Bible study.

The bottom line of the plan was for the church member to become,
at least, a prayer warrior for their neighborhood. That is a first and major
step.

As you develop a prayer ministry in your local church, don't be discouraged if not everyone gets involved. Begin praying with those who do
want to be part of an organized prayer effort. This much I do know—your
church will not have a successful small-group ministry without church
members praying for the ministry. In fact, I suggest that you have your first
small-group leadership teams come from those involved in the prayer warrior ministry.

If we pray, we will receive Holy Spirit power.

If we don't pray, we are powerless.

In the late 1980s I was part of a team that launched national training
for small-group leaders. We assumed that everyone wanting to lead small
groups already made prayer a part of their lives and that they were seeking revival and Holy Spirit power. We soon discovered that the attendees
wanted spiritual mentoring. Those attending the training sessions wanted
the experience of a Spirit-filled life, but they needed someone to mentor
them into actually realizing the experience.

Because of this, we launched the North American Prayer and Small
Group Conferences. The weeklong experience was a three-day meeting
emphasizing prayer, followed by a continual prayer and worship experience
blended into three additional days of small-group training. Some of the
participants came just for the prayer conference, and others attended just the
small-group conference. But others stayed the entire week. One man who
came just for the small-group conference approached me and said, "What

happened here during the prayer conference? I can feel the presence of the Holy Spirit in this place."

When the participants went home with a revived spiritual experience and tools to continue the experience, coupled with small-group ministry skills, God could do mighty works for His kingdom in their lives and their communities.

In conclusion

Let's be transparent. One of the reasons small groups (or any other type of outreach endeavor, for that matter) do not work in some churches is that a portion of the members are attendees, but not participants. They are noninvolved Christians. Now, I am thankful that all Christians, no matter where they are in their journey with God, are in church rather than staying home! That means there is opportunity for them to choose to become involved. As a dear friend of mine would say: "This is a good thing!"

Remember—small groups will not necessarily revive a lukewarm church, and small groups will probably struggle in a lukewarm church. A church must begin with revival and renewal before it can make an impact on the community with small groups or any other ministry event.

The bottom line: The first step in small-group ministries is to mentor your church family into becoming a praying church.

Now what?

As you think about your own church, perhaps one of these reasons discussed in this chapter can help you to understand and overcome your small-group struggles. Maybe none of these reasons apply to your situation. This much I do know—if you are still at a loss to know how to make small groups a success in your church, begin with developing a praying church and a discipleship-mentoring program, and your issues will become clearer as you present them before God. Also, why not start a small group on your own? Get started, and God will lead you.

------

[1] A. G. Daniells, Ministerial retreat address, Los Angeles, California, March 1912. Quoted in Russell Burrill, *The Life and Mission of the Local Church,* pp. 177, 178.

[2]George I. Butler, *"Assumption of Facts," Replies to Elder Canright's Attacks on Seventh-day Adventists* (Battle Creek, Mich.: Review and Herald, 1888 and 1895), p. 24. Quoted in Russell Burrill, *The Life and Mission of the Local Church,* p. 172.

[3]Ellen G. White, *Testimonies for the Church,* vol. 7, pp. 19, 20.

[4]Ellen G. White, *Fundamentals of Christian Education,* p. 207.

SECTION III:
DIGGING DEEPER

Chapter 15

EARLY CHURCH HISTORY AND ITS IMPACT ON SMALL GROUPS

It was awesome! Mind-boggling, to be exact! I had just stepped out the entrance of the Metro in Rome. About 1,000 feet away stood the ruins of the Colosseum. Begun by Vespasian shortly after A.D. 70 and opened by the ruler Titus 10 years later, it is still a spectacle to behold.

Known in its day as the Flavian Amphitheater, it stands an imposing 163 feet tall, 611 feet long, and took an estimated 100,000 cubic meters of material to build! Just the metal pins that hold the blocks together weigh more than 300 tons! When the amphitheater was opened, some 70,000 spectators could be entertained at one time. Built in an era of persecution and ritualized violence, with gladiators and wild animals of all kinds competing in deadly contests, the Colosseum has a history of death, blood, and tragedy.[1]

The Colosseum is a reminder of Rome's power and its negative view, for some time, of the "sect" known as Christianity. Although historians debate which coliseums, including the one in Rome, were actually used to put Christians to death, one thing is certain—martyrdoms occurred. Looking at the underground tunnels, wild animal pens, and elevator systems that brought man and beast together in the middle of the arena, you can almost hear and feel the fury of death. The mind's eye visualizes the roar of the crowd as another martyr, kneeling in prayer, is torn limb from limb by wild animals.

During this era house churches and home groups flourished, even though Christianity faced heavy persecution. Not only does Scripture demonstrate Satan's desire to eliminate Christianity, but historians document how the Roman Empire cooperated in this process.

Nero, a first-century Roman emperor, passed decrees inhibiting certain secret societies and new religious movements ("sects") as the emperor called them. Nero stated that Christians could not build churches or public meeting places. Violators could lose their property, Roman citizenship, and even their lives.[2] This is one of the reasons Christians first met in their homes for worship. Nero unwittingly assisted in establishing an outreach system that defeated his own desire to restrict the growth of Christianity.

Nero became a relentless persecutor of Christians. He set fire to Rome, and then blamed it on the Christians.[3] Christians who refused to renounce their faith were sewn into animal skins and ripped to pieces by wild dogs as cheering spectators watched.[4] Nero's fame as a persecutor, however, was assured when he became the first emperor to ride a chariot through his private gardens at night—by the light of human torches! He had Christian martyrs covered with oily tar and then set on fire for his enjoyment.[5]

Nero's decree against Christian church buildings lasted some 250 years (from A.D. 64 to 313), but the church continued to grow anyway, meeting in homes.[6] Emperor Trajan (A.D. 98-117) revived the decrees against secret societies. Among these, he included Christianity, which he labeled a "depraved and immoderate superstition." Consequently, the persecution the church had faced under the preceding emperor, Domitian, continued.[7]

Even though Nero, Trajan, and other Roman leaders repressed Christianity by banning public assembly, the Spirit of God was still moving. Prior to A.D. 300 there is but one historical reference to a building for Christian gatherings, and that building was in Persia outside the Roman Empire.[8]

However, the strength of the Christian home church during this time was illustrated by an incident that took place in A.D. 170. The Roman emperor issued a decree that Christians in Alexandria, the largest city in Egypt at that time, were to "desist from their faith and meetings" or Roman armies would be sent to destroy them. The bishop of Alexandria responded by stating that in order to destroy the Christians there, the Romans would have to kill more than half the city's population![9]

Christianity legalized

In the fourth century (A.D. 313) the emperor Constantine declared Christianity to be the official religion of the Roman Empire. For the time being, persecution of Christians ended, and church building projects began throughout the empire. With the headquarters of both the empire and the Christian church located in Rome, leaders of both church and state joined hands to promote the growth of Christianity.

The steps leading to Constantine's decree began in A.D. 311 in the city of Nicomedia by the Roman emperor Galerius. Galerius declared that "the purpose of reclaiming the Christians from their willful innovation and the multitude of their sects to the laws and the discipline of Roman state was not accomplished; and that he would now grant them permission to hold their religious assemblies, provided they disturbed not the order of the state."[10]

Constantine's decree in A.D. 313 went beyond that of Galerius. It was a decisive step from hostile neutrality to friendly neutrality and protection. It prepared the way for Christianity to be the legally recognized religion of the Roman Empire. Constantine's decree ordered the immediate, full restoration of all confiscated church property at the expense of the Roman treasury.[11] Following his decree, Constantine led the way in building church structures with elaborate architecture. He built magnificent Christian churches in Jerusalem, Bethlehem, and Constantinople.

Eusebius, church historian, describes a church built in Tyre between A.D. 313 and 322. It included a large porch, a quadrangular atrium surrounded by columns, a fountain in the center of the atrium for those attending to wash their hands and feet before entering, interior porticoes, galleries, altars, thrones for the bishops, and benches for the members. Building materials included cedar of Lebanon, granite, and other precious materials.[12]

The early believers, the house church, and sharing one's faith

These early Christian believers called the church a "household of faith" (Gal. 6:10). Paul offered encouragement to the young members by continually reminding them that they belonged to a spiritual family. They were members of "the household of God" (Eph. 2:19). Peter expanded the concept to describe the members as "a spiritual house" (1 Peter 2:5) in which God lived.

This metaphor edged over into reality, because, as we have previously mentioned, Christian life revolved around private homes during the first few centuries. The home became the meeting place of the early believers. Four biblical examples are the church in the house of Mary, the mother of John Mark (see Acts 12:12), the church in the house of Priscilla and Aquila (see Rom. 16:3-5; 1 Cor. 16:19), the church in the house of Philemon (see Philemon 2), and the church in the house of Nymphas (see Col. 4:15). Acts 2:41-47 indicates that the early Christian believers were a tightly knit community that shared their resources and met for Bible study, fellowship, prayer, and praise.

Clement, Church Father, describes a house meeting that he visited. "The master of the house welcomed us," he wrote, "and led us to a certain apartment, arranged like a theater, and beautifully built. There we found considerable crowds waiting for us, who had come during the night."[13]

There were a variety of types of house meetings:

- prayer meetings (Acts 12:12)
- Christian fellowship (Acts 21:7)
- common meals, possibly Communion services (Acts 2:46)
- prayer, worship, and instruction (Acts 20:7)
- impromptu evangelistic gatherings (Acts 16:32)
- planned meetings to present the gospel (Acts 10:22)
- follow-up of those inquiring about the gospel (Acts 18:26)
- organizational instruction (Acts 5:42)

There was balance between the home and public meetings and a "winning combination" in the nurture and evangelistic methods that were followed. Scripture states that after the outpouring of the Holy Spirit, the believers met daily "in the temple, and in every house, . . . teaching and preaching Jesus as the Christ" (Acts 5:42). Later we see Paul doing the same. He also taught and evangelized "from house to house" (Acts 20:20). Meetings in the homes provided the backbone of the church structure. However, the home was not the only context in which the church functioned.

Large mass meetings were also part of the early Christian evangelistic strategy. An example of this is Peter's sermon recorded in Acts 2, resulting in 3,000 believers being added to the church.

The synagogues were the "church buildings" for the Jews. At first Christians met with the Jews in the synagogue; they considered themselves to be merely a reformed group within Judaism, not a separate denomination or religion. But as Christians continued preaching and teaching, opposition from the Jewish leaders followed. Eventually Christians were barred from the synagogues and were forced to meet in private homes where neighbors could be invited to discuss spiritual topics and listen to the gospel story with less danger of being interrupted.

However, except at certain periods of intense persecution, Christians were able to witness in the marketplace. One of our Russian leaders shared with me an excellent modern-day example of marketplace evangelism. During the height of the persecution of Christians in Russia, public and private meetings of Christians were banned, especially any evangelizing. The believers worked around this as best they could. One way was to go to the open market every week.

One of our pastors took a rooster with him to the market every week and stood there with it. Other Adventist members would stand and talk with him, pretending they were discussing the purchase of the rooster. In reality they were discussing the Sabbath school lesson, church business, evangelism, or giving a Bible study. Sometimes a member would also bring something to the market to sell and would stand by the pastor with the rooster. Staring straight ahead, they would discuss church and spiritual issues. One day a KGB officer approached our pastor and said, "What is wrong with your rooster? You have brought him to the market for weeks. Many people talk to you about it and look it over, but no one buys it!" Through these and other risky methods the church grew and prospered in Russia.

The early Christians must have used similar strategies in times of persecution. Persecution cannot quench the gospel. As one of the Church Fathers stated: "The blood of Christians is seed."

▇ Legalization of Christianity—a negative effect

With the legalization of Christianity, the church's theology and practice regarding the role and function of the laity began to shift. This transition also affected house churches and home small groups. Centuries later John Wesley recognized this progression. He said, "Even in the first century the mystery of iniquity began to work in the church, culminating with the baptism of the Emperor Constantine, productive of far more evil to the church than all the ten persecutions put together. For at that time the church and state, the kingdoms of Christ and of the world, were so strangely and unnaturally blended together . . . that they will hardly ever be divided till Christ comes to reign upon earth."[14]

Some of the doctrinal weeds that sprang up during the Dark Ages of church history spawned the seeds of the Reformation. The Reformers reacted against the false teachings being insidiously forced upon the Christian church. Martin Luther, in protest, nailed his 95 theses on the door of the church in Wittenberg, Germany. He, and other fathers of the Reformation, began to call the church back to Scripture as the sole authority for belief and practice. Martin Luther dealt with such theological issues as baptism, salvation through the gift of Jesus Christ, Christ as our direct mediator, etc. Seventh-day Adventists would add to his list the clarification of the Sabbath, state of the dead, and the sanctuary message as other key doctrines that needed theological attention. But the area we wish to focus on is the involvement of the laity in ministry and the impact of small groups.

When Constantine declared Christianity to be the official religion of the Roman Empire and gave permission for churches to be built (A.D. 313), the theology of the church changed. As we have seen, the early Christians met primarily in their homes for their religious gatherings, because they had no church buildings. The apostles and other leading disciples (the equivalent of our paid clergy today) were primarily church planters, equippers of the laity for ministry, and circuit-riding preachers. Elders were appointed in the churches to do the work of overseeing the members and outreach. The elders and deacons took care of the basic, everyday needs of the church members. Public meetings were evidently held in houses, with attendance from a handful to more than 100. The Scriptures refer to house churches and mention that the disciples went from house to house. Ministry was carried out by the elders, deacons, and other church members. The pastors were "overseers"—evangelists and administrators.

The construction of church buildings under Constantine for public, corporate worship, had advantages and disadvantages. In the newly constructed basilicas the people attended church services at least once a week. A pastor or priest instructed them and directed the worship service. The pastor met the ministry needs of the members. Some members may have felt that corporate worship fulfilled their ministry obligation. Ministry involvement by the church members began to dwindle compared to the pre-church building days. This is not to negate church buildings, but to point out one of its effects—the failure of church leaders to empower members for ministry. Since Constantine, the church has never been the same.

Adventist church life versus the early church ministry paradigm

In the early days of the Seventh-day Adventist Church we followed a model of church life that was closer to the early church methodology. C. Mervyn Maxwell refers to a newspaper interview a reporter conducted with Adventist evangelist G. B. Starr during an evangelistic campaign. This interview sheds light on the Adventist model of ministry in our church's formative years. The reporter asked Starr by what means the Adventists had grown so rapidly. His answer: "We have no settled pastors. Our churches are taught largely to take care of themselves, while nearly all of our ministers work as evangelists in new fields. In the winter they go out into the churches, halls, or school house and raise up believers. In the summer we use tents, pitching them in the cities and villages where we teach the people these doctrines. This year we shall run about 100 tents in this way. Besides these, we send out large numbers of colporteurs with our tracts and books, who visit the families and teach them the Bible. Last year we employed about 125 in this manner. Bible reading is another class of work. The workers go from house to house holding Bible readings with from one to twenty individuals. Last year they gave 10,000 of such Bible readings. At the same time we had employed about 300 canvassers, constantly canvassing the country and selling our larger works. In addition to this, every church has a missionary society. Last year these numbered 10,500 members. Every one of these members does more or less missionary work, such as selling books, loaning or giving away tracts, obtaining subscriptions to our periodicals, visiting families, looking after the poor, aiding the sick, etc. Last year they made 102,000 visits, wrote 40,000 letters, obtained 38,700 subscriptions to our periodicals, distributed 15,500,000 pages of reading matter and 1,600,000 periodicals."[15]

No wonder the Adventist Church grew! We might not use exactly the same methods today, but the principle is the same—an involved and empowered laity. Ellen White wrote, "To every one work has been allotted, and no one can be a substitute for another."[16]

At a ministerial meeting in Los Angeles, California, in March 1912, A. G. Daniells, General Conference president, spoke these words: "We have not settled our ministers over churches as pastors to any large extent. In some of the very large churches we have elected pastors, but as a rule we have held ourselves ready for field service, evangelistic work, and our brethren and sisters have held themselves ready to maintain their church services and carry forward their church work without settled pastors. And I hope this will never cease to be the order of affairs in this denomination; for when we cease our forward movement work and begin to settle over our churches, to stay by them, and do their thinking and their praying and their work that is to be done, then our churches will begin to weaken, and to lose their life and spirit, and become paralyzed and fossilized and our work will be on a retreat."[17]

"Paralyzed and fossilized"—those words remind me of Ezekiel's description of the church as a valley of dry bones. A church that is inactive in ministry is a church that is dead or dying. A church that depends solely on the pastor and the leaders chosen by the nominating committee to do their ministry for them is a church that is out of harmony with God's will. As Seventh-day Adventists, we would not think of violating the Sabbath hours by improper activity, but some have fallen into Satan's trap of ignoring God's plan of taking the gospel to all the world. That plan involves every Christian involved in ministry at all times. The Bible calls this constant readiness being prepared "in season and out of season" (2 Tim. 4:2).

The first 39 pages of *Testimonies for the Church,* volume 7, highlight the way the Adventist Church grew in its first 60 years. Here was the methodology on which the growth was based:

"Just as soon as a church is organized, let the minister set the members at work. They will need to be taught how to labor successfully. Let the minister devote more of his time to educating than to preaching. Let him teach the people how to give others the knowledge they have received."[18]

"The greatest help that can be given our people is to teach them to work for God, and to depend on Him, not on the ministers. Let them learn to work as Christ worked. Let them join His army of workers and do faithful service for Him."[19]

"God has not given His ministers the work of setting the churches right. No sooner is this work done, apparently, than it has to be done over again. Church members that are thus looked after and labored for become religious weaklings. . . . God has withheld His blessings because His people have not worked in harmony with His directions."[20]

"Churches are to be organized, and plans laid for work to be done by the members of the newly organized churches. As workers go forth filled with zeal, and with the love of God, the churches at home will be revived; for the success of the workers will be regarded as a subject of deep personal concern by every member of the church."[21]

Although the job description and role of the pastor is complex in the twenty-first century, the pastor's role as equipper and mentor is essential and vital to obtain and maintain a healthy church. As society changes, so does the pastor's job description and the way we organize for mission; however, the biblical direction of the pastor as equipper should always be maintained. You see, one characteristic that never changes with time is the vital role of the pastor in the mission and work of the church. The biblical gift of pastor is a key spiritual gift mentioned in Scripture. Why? Because the pastor as a spiritual undershepherd to Jesus Christ, the true Shepherd, is essential to leading the members into a "serving" relationship with God.

Some of us have lost our passion for those who need to know Jesus. It is so easy to get caught up in the whirlwind of life that we forget our reason for being. Too many of us have left ministry to the paid clergy. We return our tithe, so the pastor can reach the lost, and we drive off to our places of employment, thinking we have done our part. That mind-set is not biblical and must be changed! We must think this way: *God has given me an occupation to earn money to sustain my family, but my primary occupation is my field of ministry. The money is secondary; lost people are primary!* This does not mean that one does not respect the rights and privacy of clientele or customers, but it does mean that each of us must pray for and look for opportunities to make a spiritual difference in the lives of men and women in our community.

Lessons from history

This review of Adventist history says to me that early on our church had intentional plans for every member to be involved in ministry. The conference leaders and pastors were intentional about equipping and encouraging all members to do *something* to tell others the story of Jesus.

This "involvement blitz" involved both one-on-one and group contact with one's neighbors and community with the goal of engaging them in Christ-centered Bible study.

Today, following a "spiritual gifts"-based theology, we can do no less (see 1 Cor. 12; Eph. 4). Our methods may be different, because of our twenty-first-century culture. However, Christians sharing the story of their friend, Jesus, with friends, neighbors, and work associates should still be the bull's-eye of our ministry target.

And what better way is there to deepen friendships and talk about the Bible than in a relaxing home environment with a group of people with similar goals? Small groups are still culturally relevant in twenty-first-century life. It was God's plan 2,000 years ago when Jesus walked upon this earth, and it is God's plan today. The question for you and me is: "What are we doing about it?"

---

[1] R. A. Staccioli, *Rome Past and Present*.
[2] Philip Schaff, *History of the Christian Church*, vol. 1, p. 384.
[3] *Ibid.*, p. 379.
[4] *Ibid.*, p. 382.
[5] *Ibid.*
[6] *Ibid.*
[7] *Ibid.*
[8] Albert J. Wollen, *Miracles Happen in Group Bible Study*, p. 30.
[9] *Ibid.*, p. 29.
[10] Schaff, vol. 2, p. 71.
[11] *Ibid.*, p. 72.
[12] *Ibid.*, pp. 198–202.
[13] Michael Green, *Evangelism in the Early Church*, p. 208.
[14] Quoted by William Beckham, "The Two-winged Church Will Fly," *Seminar Notebook* (1996), p. 18.
[15] Quoted in Russell Burrill, *Revolution in the Church*, p. 39.
[16] Ellen G. White, *Christian Service*, p. 10.
[17] Quoted in Burrill, p. 41.
[18] Ellen G. White, *Testimonies for the Church*, vol. 7, p. 20.
[19] *Ibid.*, p. 19.
[20] *Ibid.*, p. 18.
[21] Ellen G. White, *Gospel Workers* p. 26.

Chapter 16

THE ADVENTIST CHURCH AND SMALL GROUPS

The Seventh-day Adventist Church grew out of the Millerite movement of the 1840s, which drew adherents from several mainline Christian denominations. One of these was the Methodist Church. Ellen White was baptized into the Methodist Church in 1842. She described the event in these words: "It was a windy day when we, twelve in number, went down into the sea to be baptized. The waves ran high and dashed upon the shore, but as I took up this heavy cross, my peace was like a river. When I arose from the water, my strength was nearly gone, for the power of the Lord rested upon me. I felt that henceforth I was not of this world, but had risen from the watery grave into a newness of life. The same day in the afternoon I was received into the church in full membership."[1]

As a member of the Methodist Church, Ellen White became involved in what were called "class meetings."[2] Class meetings originated in England among the Methodists and later developed into the weekly prayer meeting that has found its way into many Christian denominations, including the Seventh-day Adventist Church. In order to understand the background of these meetings, we must go back to England in the nineteenth century and review the ministry of John Wesley, the founder of the Methodist Church.

In the years following the Reformation, Christianity continued to enjoy popular acceptance, but church institutional formality returned. Because of this, home group meetings withered, and the influence of Christianity declined in the face of the European Industrial Revolution in the early eighteenth century. But God used John Wesley and George Whitefield to spearhead a spiritual revival in England.

Wesley and Whitefield traveled the English countryside, calling people back to God. As individuals made decisions for Christ, they were organized into societies. These societies met together in rented facilities for prayer, Bible study, fellowship, and worship.[3]

In Bristol a problem arose in various societies concerning how to raise money to pay the monthly rent for a public meeting place. Wesley divided the societies into groups of 12. He assigned a leader in each group to collect a penny every week from each family to pay the rent. As leaders collected the pennies, they reported to Wesley that they were discovering among the group members drinking problems, marriage difficulties, and other situations that shouldn't be part of a Christian lifestyle.

After this revelation, the collection plan was revised. The 12 group members began to meet in one of the members' houses, and they began to discuss openly their personal problems for mutual edification.[4]

The spiritual and personal growth in the lives of these group members was phenomenal. Word of the positive influence of the Bristol societies traveled to London. Within a short time the London society also divided into groups of 12. From this simple beginning came the Methodist class meetings. These groups provided Bible study, prayer, testimonies, and fellowship. The Wesleyan revival in England flourished as a result of this group process. It was a revival led by lay members—not paid clergy, but lay members—opening the Bible in homes all across England.

Wesley's movement (called Methodism because Wesley followed specific methods to accomplish ministry) eventually jumped the Atlantic. Churches were built, and public meetings combined with the small-class meetings provided the basis for the growth of Methodism in the United States.[5]

The small-group movement within Methodism had an impact on the Seventh-day Adventist Church because of the influence of Ellen White. In her youth Ellen White became involved in the Millerite movement and the subsequent formation of the Seventh-day Adventist Church. Early in her experience she recognized the positive spiritual benefits of small-group ministry. Consequently, she penned the following under God's direction:

"Preach less, and educate more, by holding Bible-readings, and by praying with families and little companies.

"To all who are working with Christ I would say, Wherever you can gain access to the people by the fireside, improve your opportunity. Take your Bible, and open before them its great truths. Your success will not depend so much upon your knowledge and accomplishments, as upon your ability to find your way to the heart. By being social and coming close to the people, you may turn the current of their thoughts more readily than by the most able discourse. The presentation of Christ in the family, by the fireside, and in small gatherings in private houses, is often more successful in winning souls to Jesus than are sermons delivered in the open air, to the moving throng, or even in halls or churches."[6]

"Let small companies assemble together in the evening or early morning to study the Bible for themselves. Let them have a season of prayer that they may be strengthened and enlightened and sanctified by the Holy Spirit. . . .

"If you will do this, a great blessing will come to you from the One who gave His whole life to service, the One who redeemed you by His own life. . . . What testimonies you should bear of the loving acquaintance you have made with your fellow workers in these precious seasons when seeking the blessing of God. Let each tell his experience in simple words. . . .

"Let little companies meet together to study the Scriptures. You will lose nothing by this, but will gain much."[7]

Ellen White had another opportunity to observe the impact of small groups upon a country and a city. From 1891 to 1900 she was in Australia, assisting with the development of the Seventh-day Adventist Church there, particularly the establishment of Avondale College. While in Australia, she wrote several books, including *The Desire of Ages* and *Steps to Christ*.

I believe God placed Ellen White in Australia for another significant reason. She had already experienced firsthand the power of small groups. Now God was placing her in a country where a small-group revival was taking place. This would provide an opportunity to reinforce the spiritual power of small-group ministries in her mind and experience.

In Australia during the 1890s events took place that were related to what is known today as the "Welsh Revival." The clergy in and around Melbourne met together to pray for the spiritual health of their members and colleagues. The pastors gained so much strength from this time together that they decided the best thing they could do for their members' spiritual well-being was to organize them into similar groups for Bible study, prayer, and fellowship. Consequently, at the peak of the revival 2,000 home meetings were occurring weekly in the city. The Melbourne pastors involved in small-group ministry invited R. A. Torrey to come from America and conduct an evangelistic campaign in their city. The result was a tremendous revival.

A young woman from Wales was visiting Melbourne at this time and became caught up in the revival. She took her spiritual experience back to Wales when she returned and began helping with the cottage prayer meetings there. These meeting contributed to the Welsh Revival, which had a tremendous impact on the growth of Christianity in Wales.[8]

At this same time God emphasized to Ellen White the importance of small-group ministry, and she began to write on the topic:

"The formation of small companies as a basis of Christian effort is a plan that has been presented before me by One who cannot err. If there is a large number in the church, let the members be formed into small companies, to work not only for the church members but for unbelievers also."[9]

"But on such occasions as our annual camp meetings we must never lose sight of the opportunities afforded for teaching the believers how to do practical missionary work. . . where they may live. In many instances it would be well to set apart certain men to carry the burden of different lines of educational work at these meetings. Let some help the people to learn how to give Bible readings and to conduct cottage meetings. Let others bear the burden of teaching the people how to practice the principles of health and temperance, and how to give treatments to the sick. Still others may labor in the interests of our periodical and book work."[10]

"Let the teachers in our schools devote Sunday to missionary effort. Let them take the students with them to hold meetings for those who know not the truth. Sunday can be used for carrying forward various lines of work that will accomplish much for the Lord. On this day house-to-house work can be done. Open-air meetings and cottage meetings can be held."[11]

As can be seen through church history and the pen of Ellen White, God has eternal purposes in mind to be accomplished through small groups. As God revealed events that would occur before the second coming of Jesus, it became clear that small groups and sharing the Scriptures with our neighbors are an important part of His plan for preparing the world for that great event.

"In visions of the night, representations passed before me of a great reformatory movement among God's people. Many were praising God. The sick were healed, and other miracles were wrought. A spirit of intercession was seen, even as was manifested before the great Day of Pentecost. Hundreds and thousands were seen visiting families and opening before them the Word of God. Hearts were convicted by the power of the Holy Spirit, and a spirit of genuine conversion was manifest. On every side doors were thrown open to the proclamation of the truth. The world seemed to be lightened with the heavenly influence. Great blessings were received by the true and humble people of God. I heard voices of thanksgiving and praise, and there seemed to be a reformation such as we witnessed in 1844."[12]

"I saw the saints leaving the cities and villages, and associating together in companies, and living in the most solitary places. Angels provided them food and water, while the wicked were suffering from hunger and thirst."[13]

Ellen White uses such phrases as "cottage meeting," "small companies," "little companies," and "small gatherings" to refer to what we call "small groups." Consider the elements of her counsel:

1. God told her that large churches should have small groups.

2. Small groups commonly meet in "private houses."

3. Small groups meet by the "fireside."

4. Small groups meet in the evening or morning, whichever is convenient for one's schedule.

5. The purpose of these meetings is to minister to baptized "church members," win "souls to Jesus," and to minister to "unbelievers."

6. What is done during these meetings? She says members are to (a) "open your Bibles," "study the Bible," "present Christ," conduct "Bible readings"; (b) pray; (c) "be social," "come close to the people," "find your way to the heart," and (d) "share testimonies."

Ellen White's comments concerning small-group life reflect very closely the elements of Acts 2:42-47, which include Bible study, home fellowship, prayer, food, and outreach.

Types of Adventist meetings

Ellen White used several terms to describe various types of meetings in the Adventist Church. The terminology and practice has varied somewhat over the years, but the principles remain the same.

1. Cottage meetings. These were small groups meeting during the week for Bible study, prayer, fellowship, and sharing testimonies. The emphasis was on Bible study. The groups usually met in homes. They followed a format that reached out to both church members and unbelievers. "Little companies" and "small companies" appear to refer to these cottage meetings.

2. Bible readings. C. Mervyn Maxwell, Adventist historian, states that the first Bible reading in the Adventist Church occurred as the result of a storm during a camp meeting in California. When the noise of the storm made preaching impractical, someone picked up a Bible and began asking questions along a doctrinal theme, inviting the congregation to look up the texts that answered the questions. This simple question-and-answer method caught on and became quite popular. Eventually a call went out for people to send in their favorite Bible readings. In 1888 the best of these were compiled into the first edition of *Bible Readings for the Home Circle.*

Evidently a Bible reading was similar to what we would call a seminar or a workshop. At times Ellen White's references to church members giving Bible readings seems to indicate that this is something different than meeting in small companies. At other times it appears as if the two are taking place simultaneously. Evidently homes were used not only for small-group meetings but also for a Bible lecture series similar to seminars conducted today, such as Revelation seminars, Discover Jesus seminars, etc.

Earlier I referred to a newspaper interview in Indiana with Adventist evangelist G. B. Starr, in which Starr explained Bible readings: "Bible reading is another class of work," he told the reporter. "The workers go from house to house holding Bible readings with from one to twenty individuals. Last year they gave 10,000 of such Bible readings."[14] Apparently a Bible reading involved as few people or as many as would fit into a home.

3. Social meetings.[15] In the mid-nineteenth century the Methodist class meeting changed into a weekly prayer meeting that included social dimensions. The Adventist Church also eventually included a social meeting as part of its services. The social meeting was sometimes held after a preaching service, sometimes at midweek, but frequently on Sabbath. The social meeting allowed church members time to share the personal benefit they had received from the sermon or Bible study presentation. At other times the social meeting was held in lieu of a sermon, since early Adventists did not have regular assigned pastors. The meeting followed Sabbath school.

The social meeting included prayer, testimonies, words of encouragement to one another, singing, and fellowship. It was similar to the elements contained in what we would call a praise, prayer, and testimony service. One difference was that the social meeting was not limited to a certain number. In some cases, if the congregation was too large, the participants would divide into smaller groups to give everyone an opportunity to participate.

James White, early Adventist pioneer and husband of Ellen White, provides us with a glimpse of an effective social meeting:

"Social meetings were marked with great solemnity. Sins were confessed with tears, and there was a general breaking down before God, and strong pleadings for pardon, and a fitness to meet the Lord at His coming. And the humble disciples of the Lord did not seek His face in vain. Before that meeting closed, hundreds testified with tears of joy that they had sought the Lord and found Him, and had tasted the sweets of sins forgiven."[16]

"During one social meeting 117 testimonies were given in 53 minutes. All right to the point."[17] A review of early Adventist articles and letters demonstrates that the social meeting was a key part of church life; some even considered attendance to be a duty. The social meeting was a time to build community among the members through prayer and testimonies. Ellen White said that it was essential for the church to have social meetings and that young ministers should be taught how to conduct them.[18] In 1882 she described the social meeting in these words:

"The prayer and social meetings should be the most interesting gatherings that are held. Plans should be laid, and wisdom sought of God, to conduct these meetings so that they will be interesting and attractive. The people hunger for the bread of life. If they find it at the prayer-meeting, they will go there to receive it. Long, prosy talks and prayers are out of place anywhere, and especially in the social meeting. They weary the angels as well as the people who listen to them. Our prayers should be short, and right to the point. Let the Spirit of God pervade the hearts of the worshipers, and it will sweep away all formality and dullness."[19]

The social meeting in the Adventist Church evolved into the prayer meeting that gradually changed from the original plan of prayer, praise, and testimony to a pastoral sermon followed by a few minutes of prayer. Today some churches don't even have a prayer meeting. If they do, only a few attend. We need to go back to the original format, which involves a more relational approach. Some of the prayer conferences of the past two decades closely reflect the characteristics of the social meeting.

4. *Open-air meetings/camp meetings.* Leading people to accept Jesus and Bible truth has always been an Adventist priority. Early Adventists preached

wherever and whenever there was opportunity. Because of a lack of funds to rent public buildings and because large public facilities often were not available, meetings were conducted outside. An example was an evangelistic meeting held in May 1854 at Locke, Michigan. "The schoolhouse they used would not hold half the audience, so the speaker stood in the open window and spoke both to those in the house and to a larger crowd on the grass and in their carriages."[20] Sometimes large crowds would gather on the property of someone's farm or in a central public gathering place.

Using tents for public meetings was a novelty, especially in the western United States in the mid-1800s. One could attract a crowd simply by putting up a tent. Thus, tents and open-air meetings were very successful. The first Seventh-day Adventist camp meeting was held in 1868 in a maple grove on the farm of Elder E. H. Root, at Wright, Michigan. It was an outdoor meeting using both open-air seating and tents. "The earlier camp meetings were planned not alone for the spiritual blessing of believers but as evangelistic efforts for the general public; therefore, it was the policy to change the place of meeting each year; and much of the preaching, especially in the evening and on Sunday, was with this purpose in mind. This plan was advocated by Mrs. White as late as 1900."[21]

5. *Sabbath worship services.* The Sabbath worship services were a vital part of Adventism. These usually involved a Sabbath school composed of Bible study, prayer, and fellowship, with outreach and learning leadership skills. The service that followed was a preaching service or a social meeting.

6. *Personal visitation.* Today we sometimes use the phrase "friendship evangelism" to describe what was earlier called "personal visitation." The key ingredients involve establishing social relationships with attending nonmembers, neighbors, and work associates, with the goal of meeting their needs and introducing them to Jesus through Bible study and personal experience.

7. *Personal prayer and Bible study.* The Bible states that Jesus spent much time in prayer. If Christians are to grow spiritually or have an effective ministry, they must spend time daily with God.

A local church that incorporates these seven items will have a balanced program of nurture and outreach. There will be opportunities for the Holy Spirit to make an impact on such a ministry. Not only will the Spirit move and act in the personal lives of the members, but He will change lives as

God's plans are followed. Ellen White stated it well when she said, "Surrender all your plans to Him [God], to be carried out or given up as His providence shall indicate. Thus day by day you may be giving your life into the hands of God, and thus your life will be molded more and more after the life of Christ."[22]

A friend of mine who pastors in the Pacific Northwest was excited about the baptisms and increasing number of small groups in his church. My friend told me that usually he has to encourage new groups to start. However, now his members have seen the benefit of small groups. Following a reaping meeting, one of the men in his church said, "We must place the new members and interests in small groups. We don't have enough groups, so we need to start three more." Other members followed his lead and, on their own, organized enough groups to meet the church's needs. My pastor friend told me that it was exciting to watch his members take the lead. The equipping, mentoring, and vision-casting had paid off!

NOTE: For information on how to lead a social meeting, see Ellen G. White, *Testimonies for the Church,* volume 2, pages 577-582. The information shared is also helpful in leading small-group meetings.

---

[1] Ellen G. White, *Life Sketches,* p. 25.

[2] *Ibid.,* p. 43.

[3] John Dillenberger and Claude Welch, *Protestant Christianity,* pp. 129-136.

[4] B. Waugh and T. Mason, *The Works of the Reverend John Wesley,* vol. 7, p. 12.

[5] A. J. Wollen, *Miracles Happen in Group Bible Study,* p. 36.

[6] Ellen G. White, *Gospel Workers,* p. 193.

[7] Ellen G. White, *This Day With God,* p. 11.

[8] Wollen, pp. 36, 37.

[9] Ellen G. White, *Evangelism,* p. 115.

[10] Ellen G. White, *Testimonies for the Church,* vol. 9, pp. 82, 83.

[11] Ellen G. White, *Counsels to Parents, Teachers, and Students,* p. 551.

[12] Ellen G. White, *Testimonies for the Church,* vol. 9, p. 126.

[13] Ellen G. White, *Early Writings,* p. 282.

[14] G. B. Starr, in Wabash, Indiana, *Plain Dealer,* Oct. 1, 1886, p. 5.

[15] Much of this information concerning social meetings is taken from a research project by Russell Burrill, *A Biblical and Adventist Historical Study of Small Groups as a Basis for Mission.*

[16] James White, *Life Incidents,* vol. 1, pp. 167, 168. Here James White is speaking of social meetings during the Millerite movement.

[17] J. N. Loughborough, *Miracles in My Life,* p. 88.

[18] Ellen G. White, in *Signs of the Times,* May 17, 1883.

[19] Ellen G. White, in *Review and Herald,* Oct. 10, 1882.

[20] Arthur W. Spalding, *Origin and History of Seventh-day Adventists,* vol. 2, p. 7.

[21] *Ibid.,* pp. 17, 19.

[22] Ellen G. White, *Steps to Christ,* p. 70.

Chapter 17

LAUGH, SARAH, LAUGH

I had read the story and the Bible verse many times, but a seminar instructor brought it to my attention again—"Sarah laughed" (Gen. 18:12). Sarah laughed at God's plan for her. As I went back and reread Genesis 17 and 18, I began to reflect on the lessons from the story of Abraham and Sarah for God's church today.

Terah, Abraham's father, lived to the ripe old age of 205 years (see Gen. 11:32). Based on this standard, Abraham was still a youngster at 75 years of age when God told him to pack up his household and move to Canaan. Some 24 years later (see Gen. 17:1) God told Abraham that His word was still good—the promise that Abraham would become a great nation, made to him at 75 years of age, was still good when he was 99. Sarah, God affirmed, would have a son from whom He would make a great nation.

I can picture the scene in my mind. Abraham looks up at God, and a huge smile crosses his face. He laughingly says, with his shoulders heaving from his laughter, "Surely, God, You have to be kidding! I am 99, and Sarah is 90! Her child-bearing years are over!"

God interrupts Abraham, and I imagine Him smiling back and saying, "I'm serious, Abraham. I am God, and nothing is impossible for Me. In fact, I waited this long to fulfill My promise, because I wanted you to see that this is a 'God-thing,' not a 'man-thing.' Normal biological processes won't work this time. It will take a miracle; it will take Me" (see verses 15-22).

Sometime later, around lunchtime, three heavenly beings visited Abraham. Following the custom of the day, Sarah was standing behind the tent curtains. Women were forbidden to mingle freely with men, including male guests, especially if they were strangers. However, Bedouin women could usually be found close to the opening of the tent, just out of view, so they could hear the conversation and know what was going on.

The mention of Sarah's name must have surprised her and Abraham as well. The Bible simply says, "Sarah laughed within herself" (Gen. 18:12). In other words, Sarah's laugh and her comment about her age were not audible—or at best, barely audible. In fact, she was so surprised that God knew her thoughts and barely spoken words that she denied even saying them when confronted about it! (See verses 13-15.)

Sarah laughed, not at *God,* but at the impossibility, the improbability, of giving birth to a son. It appears that she believed God's promise of a great nation, but His promise that she would give birth to a son was another matter.

Before we are too hard on Sarah, however, let's remember that we sometimes laugh at God too. As we get older, the enthusiasm and ideas of our youth in the church sometimes cause us to laugh, smile, or even frown. It is easy to settle back in our pew and be comfortable. Normally, the older we get, the less we like change. Either we have tried everything or seen everything tried. The early vision of our youth tends to fade over time. It is easy to let the roadblocks of traditionalism, political agendas, budgets, position, committees, and other human considerations replace our vision, faith, and desire to be part of the generation that is alive when Jesus returns to this earth.

But God has always had a remnant—those followers who believe in what others call the impossible. There have always been Calebs and Joshuas. There have always been the Abrahams and Sarahs, who smile or laugh at the thought of the impossible, but who still move forward in faith, believing that God's plan will be accomplished "not by might nor by power, but by [God's] Spirit" (Zech. 4:6).

I imagine they laughed at Jesus, Peter, Paul, and John in the beginning. Luther, Wesley, and Zwingli were viewed as heretics and thorns in the flesh of the established church; these rebels simply needed to be exterminated, church leaders argued, and life would return to normal. The status quo smiled at these upstarts and sent armies and church councils against them. But it did not matter. A revolution was under way—a revolution for God that turned into a movement.

Now Sarah, once a young bride, is old. Is it possible to bring new life out of the old body? God thinks so! God looks at you and me. He sees a church scarred and challenged, and He not only believes, but He *knows* that He can bring new life into His people, His church.

Some who go by the name of "Christian" will always smile at the mention of a revival, the birth of a spiritual movement, the new methodologies, and hopes, and faith of committed believers. The status quo will always think that reality will settle back in, given some time.

But God knows different. God showed that He understood the concerns of Abraham and Sarah. He showed that He, too, has a sense of humor. For God named Sarah's promised baby boy *Isaac,* which means "laughter" (see Gen. 21:6). Not negative laughter, but joyous laughter! There is *joy* at the birth of a new age, a generation that believes and embodies the promises of God.

Not only was Abraham a man of faith, but he was a friend of God. He also had a love for people—those who would be lost eternally if no one shared with them the message of the gospel. We see this in Abraham's pleading for Sodom and Gomorrah (see Gen. 18:16-33).

God wants the same spirit and love for souls to be part of the warp and fiber of your life and mine. Like Abraham, we should have a hatred of sin, but pity and love for the sinner. All around us people are going down to a ruin as hopeless and terrible as that which befell Sodom. As God's church, our task is to introduce our friends and neighbors to Jesus so they can become fully devoted disciples, living an abundant life today with the assurance of eternal life.

Small groups are a powerful mechanism to accomplish the mission of God's church in the world today. Small groups, as we have seen, embody a biblically based, God-given methodology. Small group ministry incorporates the elements for developing disciples—friendship, support, Bible study, prayer, equipping, and sharing Jesus Christ. It is a complete discipling package. It's time for the discussion to end; it's time to launch your small group. Why not get involved today?

BIBLIOGRAPHY

Books

Anderson, Leith. *A Church for the Twenty-first Century.* Minneapolis: Bethany House, 1992.

Arnold, Jeffrey. *The Big Book on Small Groups.* Downers Grove, Ill.: InterVarsity Press, 1992.

Barclay, William. *The Gospel of John.* Philadelphia: Westminster Press, 1975.

Barker, Steve, et al. *Good Things Come in Small Groups.* Downers Grove, Ill.: InterVarsity Press, 1985.

———. *Small Group Leader's Handbook.* Downers Grove, Ill.: InterVarsity Press, 1982.

Barna, George. *Evangelism That Works.* Ventura, Calif.: Regal Books, 1995.

———. *The Power of Vision.* Ventura, Calif.: Regal Books, 1992.

Beckham, William. *The Second Reformation.* Houston: Touch Publications, Inc., 1995.

———. *The Two-winged Church Will Fly.* Houston: Touch Outreach Ministries, 1994.

———. *Where Are We Now?* Houston: Touch Global Publications, 2004.

Blackaby, Henry, and Richard Blackaby. *Spiritual Leadership.* Nashville: Broadman and Holman, 2001.

Burrill, Russell. *A Biblical and Adventist Historical Study of Small Groups as a Biblical Mission.* Berrien Springs, Mich.: Andrews University Press, 1996.

———. *The Life and Mission of the Local Church.* Fallbrook, Calif.: Hart Research Center, 1998.

———. *Revolution in the Church.* Fallbrook, Calif.: Hart Research Center, 1993.

————. *The Revolutionized Church of the 21st Century.* Fallbrook, Calif.: Hart Research Center, 1997.

Cerna, Miguel Angel. *The Power of Small Groups in the Church.* Newbury Park, Calif.: El Camino Publishing, 1991.

Chambers, Oswald. *My Utmost for His Highest.* New York: Dodd, Mead and Co., 1961.

Comiskey, Joel. *Cell Church Solutions.* Moreno Valley, Calif.: CCS Publishing, 2005.

Davis, Deena. *Discipleship Journal's 101 Best Small Group Ideas.* Colorado Springs, Colo.: NavPress, 1982.

Dillenberger, John, and Claude Welch. *Protestant Christianity.* New York: Charles Scribner and Sons, 1954.

Donahue, Bill. *Leading Life-changing Small Groups.* Grand Rapids: Zondervan, 2002.

————, and Greg Bowman. *Coaching Life-changing Small Group Leaders.* Grand Rapids: Zondervan, 2006.

————, and Russ Robinson. *Building a Church of Small Groups.* Grand Rapids: Zondervan, 2001.

Earley, Dave. *8 Habits of Effective Small Group Leaders.* Houston: Cell Group Resources, 2001.

Finnell, David. *Life in His Body.* Houston: Touch Publications, Inc., 1995.

Galloway, Dale, and Kathi Mills. *The Small Group Book.* Grand Rapids: Fleming H. Revell, 1995.

George, Carl F. *Prepare Your Church for the Future.* Tarrytown, N.Y.: Fleming H. Revell, 1991.

————, and Warren Bird. *The Coming Church Revolution.* Grand Rapids: Fleming H. Revell, 1994.

Green, Michael. *Evangelism in the Early Church.* Grand Rapids: Eerdmans, 1970.

————. *Evangelism Then and Now.* Downers Grove, Ill.: InterVarsity Press, 1979.

Greenleaf, Robert K. *Servant Leadership.* New York: Paulist Press, 1977.

Greenough, Jeanie Ashley Bates. *A Year of Beautiful Thoughts.* New York: Crowell, 1902.

Hamlin, Judy. *The Small Group Leader's Training Course, Participant's Manual.* Colorado Springs, Colo.: NavPress, 1990.

————. *The Small Group Leader's Training Course, Trainer's Manual.* Colorado Springs, Colo.: NavPress, 1990.

Hestenes, Roberta. *Using the Bible in Groups.* Philadelphia: Westminster Press, 1983.

Hipp, Jeanne. *How to Start and Grow Small Groups in Your Church.* Monrovia, Calif.: Church Growth., Inc., 1989.

Hunter, George C. *How to Reach Secular People.* Nashville: Abingdon Press, 1992.

Icenogle, Gareth Weldon. *Biblical Foundations for Small Group Ministry.* Downers Grove, Ill.: InterVarsity Press, 1994.

Jacks, Bob, and Betty Jacks. *Your Home a Lighthouse.* Colorado Springs, Colo.: NavPress, 1986.

Johnson, Kurt. *Small Group Outreach.* Hagerstown, Md.: Review and Herald, 1991.

————. *Small Groups for the End Time.* Hagerstown, Md.: Review and Herald, 1997.

Kittel, Gerhard. *Theological Dictionary of the New Testament.* Grand Rapids: Eerdmans, 1968.

Kreider, Larry. *House to House.* Houston: Touch Publications, Inc., 1995.

Lacy, Robert. *Ford: The Man and the Machine.* New York: Little Brown, 1986.

Logan, Robert E. *Beyond Church Growth.* Grand Rapids: Fleming H. Revell, 1989, 1994.

Loughborough, J. N. *Miracles in My Life.* Phoenix: Leaves of Autumn Books, 1987.

Maxwell, John C. *Developing the Leaders Around You.* Nashville: Thomas Nelson, 1995.

————. *Developing the Leader Within You.* Nashville: Thomas Nelson, 1993.

————. *The 21 Irrefutable Laws of Leadership.* Nashville: Thomas Nelson, 1998.

McBride, Neal F. *How to Build a Small Group Ministry.* Colorado Springs, Colo.: NavPress, 1995.

————. *How to Lead Small Groups.* Colorado Springs, Colo.: NavPress, 1990.

Navigators. *How to Lead Small Group Bible Studies.* Colorado Springs, Colo.: NavPress, 1982.

————. *Twelve Steps to Leading Better Bible Studies.* Colorado Springs, Colo.: NavPress, 1982.

Neighbour, Ralph W., Jr. *Where Do We Go From Here?* Houston: Touch Publications, Inc., 1990.

———. *The Seven Last Words of the Church*. Grand Rapids: Zondervan, 1973.

Neighbour, Randall. *The Naked Truth About Small Group Ministry*. Houston: Touch Publications, 2009.

Nichol, F. D., ed. *The Seventh-day Adventist Bible Commentary*. Washington, D.C.: Review and Herald, 1953.

Peace, Richard. *Small Group Evangelism*. Downers Grove, Ill.: InterVarsity Press, 1995.

Richards, Lawrence O., and Clyde Hoeldtke. *A Theology of Church Leadership*. Grand Rapids: Zondervan, 1989.

Samaan, Philip G. *Christ's Way of Reaching People*. Hagerstown, Md.: Review and Herald, 1990.

Schaff, Philip. *History of the Christian Church*. Grand Rapids: Eerdmans, 1959.

Schilt, W. Clarence. *Dynamic Small Groups*. Hagerstown, Md.: Review and Herald, 1992.

Spalding, Arthur W. *Origin and History of Seventh-day Adventists*. Washington, D.C.: Review and Herald, 1962.

Staccioli, R. A. *Rome Past and Present*. Rome: Tipolitografica CS–Padova, 2001.

Waugh, B., and T. Mason. *The Works of the Reverend John Wesley,* 1832.

White, Ellen G. *Christian Service*. Washington, D.C.: Review and Herald, 1925.

———. *Counsels to Parents, Teachers, and Students*. Mountain View, Calif.: Pacific Press, 1943.

———. *Early Writings*. Washington, D.C.: Review and Herald, 1882.

———. *Evangelism*. Washington, D.C.: Review and Herald, 1946.

———. *Fundamentals of Christian Education*. Nashville: Southern, 1923.

———. *Gospel Workers*. Washington, D.C.: Review and Herald, 1915.

———. *Life Sketches*. Mountain View, Calif.: Pacific Press, 1915.

———. *The Ministry of Healing*. Mountain View, Calif.: Pacific Press, 1905.

———. *Patriarchs and Prophets*. Mountain View, Calif.: Pacific Press, 1958.

———. *Steps to Christ*. Mountain View, Calif.: Pacific Press, 1956.

———. *Testimonies for the Church*. Mountain View, Calif.: Pacific Press, 1948.

———. *This Day With God*. Washington, D.C.: Review and Herald, 1979.

White, James. *Life Incidents.* Battle Creek, Mich.: Steam Press of the Seventh-day Adventist Publishing Association, 1868.

Williams, Dan. *Seven Myths About Small Groups.* Downers Grove, Ill.: InterVarsity Press, 1991.

Williams, Garrie F. *Ministerial Continuing Education.* Silver Spring, Md.: General Conference Ministerial Association, 1991.

Wollen, Albert J. *Miracles Happen in Group Bible Study.* Glendale, Calif.: G/L Regal Books, 1976.

Youssef, Michael. *The Leadership Style of Jesus.* Wheaton, Ill.: Victor Books, 1986.

Periodicals

Christian Education Journal
Current Thoughts and Trends
Plain Dealer (Wabash, Indiana)
Review and Herald
Signs of the Times

Papers

"Child Care Arrangements of Working Mothers in the United States." Washington, D.C.: U.S. Government Printing Office, 1968.

"Households by Presence and Number of Children Under Age Eighteen, 1950 to 1998." Demographics of the U.S.: Trends and Projections Report.

"Women's Labor Force Attachment Patterns and Maternity Leave: A Review of the Literature." U.S. Bureau of the Census, January 1999.

"Working Moms Carve Out Their Own Office Space." SourceLine Media.

QUICK START

I recommend that you read this entire book before you begin your small group, but if you are already an experienced small-group member or leader, or if you need a quick summary to get started, then this section may be helpful.

Introduction: What is a small group?

A small group is an intentional, face-to-face gathering of three to 12 people, meeting on a regular schedule, with the common purpose of developing relationships, meeting the members' felt needs, growing spiritually, and laying plans to lead others to accept Jesus as Lord and Savior of their lives.

Step 1: Organize your small-group team

There are three team positions for your group leadership team: leader, assistant leader, and host/hostess.

The small-group leader is the person appointed and recognized to serve the group by facilitating and enabling the group to achieve its purposes and goals. The leader needs to be a facilitator of group discussion and personal relationships more than an authority or distributor of information.

The leader will:

- attend a leadership training workshop, read a book such as this one, and, if possible, participate in a small group as an assistant leader or participant prior to taking on the responsibility of being a small-group leader.
- facilitate the weekly group meeting.
- oversee all details of group life in and outside of the weekly meeting.
- model and encourage participation, sharing, acceptance, and understanding among the members.

- guide the group in developing a group agreement (or covenant), goals, and in carrying out the goals that are set.
- check on members who are absent from the meeting in order to encourage them, meet their needs, and to be aware of any difficulties in their lives.
- talk and pray weekly about the group with the assistant leader and with the host.
- seek assistance as needed to ensure positive group life.
- attend regular scheduled leaders' meetings.

The assistant leader should:
- support and encourage the leader through prayer and other means.
- facilitate the group meeting when the leader is absent.
- assist in recruiting new members and following up absent members.
- assist with details such as child-care arrangements, completing and turning in required report forms, and other details as needed.
- attend regularly scheduled leaders' meetings.
- be an apprentice in training to lead a group of their own in the future.

The host should:
- provide a comfortable home or location for the meeting.
- arrange seating in the meeting room, adjust the temperature as needed, oversee refreshments if the group has them, and make sure extra Bibles, paper, study guides, pencils, etc., are available.
- answer the door and welcome the members as they arrive.
- make sure the members' needs are met—directing them to the location of the bathroom, telephone, drinking glasses, etc.
- take care of any distractions that may occur during the group meeting such as the doorbell, telephone, children, pets, etc.

Step 2: Choose a place to meet

Choosing the location of your group is critical to its success. An uncomfortably cold or warm room, noisy children, or pets can distract group members. In selecting a location, choose wisely. Careful planning should provide:

- a comfortable atmosphere in the living room or around the kitchen table. If your meeting is held at a place of business, a coffee shop, or a similar location, then choose a corner, committee room, or other site that provides as much privacy as possible.
- good lighting. This is necessary for study and developing a warm atmosphere.
- seating in a circle, so everyone can see one another as they talk.
- a location with the fewest distractions and interruptions possible. Children, pets, telephones, television, radios, etc., can disrupt your study group.
- child care if necessary in order for some group members to attend. If a home has the space, a volunteer may be found to take care of the children during the group meeting.

Step 3: Choose your study materials

Select your study materials depending on the type of group you are starting. Various study guides and other materials are available at Adventist Book Centers or local Christian bookstores. Materials by the author of this book include:

- *Peace Is an Inside Job* (felt needs), Review and Herald, 1995.
- *PrayerWorks* (prayer), Review and Herald, 1993, 2001.
- *LifeLine*, books 1 and 2 (Bible doctrines), Review and Herald, 1995.
- *Face to Face With Jesus* (the life of Jesus), Review and Herald, 1998.
- *Focus on Prophecy* (studies on Daniel and Revelation), Voice of Prophecy, 2000.

Step 4: Invite people to attend your group

The key to a successful small group is to personally invite people with whom you are acquainted.

Invite your neighbors, friends, work associates, relatives, dentist, service station attendant, hairdresser, store clerk, and other general acquaintances.

The invitation may take the form of a personal visit, a telephone call, or a handwritten or printed invitation.

Less-personal methods of invitation may also be used. For example, you may distribute a handbill advertising the types of groups available and inviting the public to attend a single organizational meeting or to call for more information.

Another method is to place a sign in your front yard advertising the meeting.

A relaxed, nonthreatening approach is the best. Say something like this: "Sue, I'm having a small-group meeting in my home on Tuesday evenings, and I want to invite you to come try it out. Several of us are studying the life of Jesus in the Gospels. We're looking for things to help us in dealing with everyday issues of life. I would like you to be a part of the group. Come this Tuesday night, and if you think it's for you, I'd like you to keep coming. If it doesn't meet your needs for now, that's OK too. What do you think?" Then hand the individual a printed invitation.

Step 5: Opening night

On the first night, have the assistant leader and host (if you have one) meet with you before the meeting begins. Once the room is prepared and the details are in order, have a season of prayer together. Basic preparation includes:

- turning on the outside house lights if it is dark outside.
- taping the welcome poster on the front door.
- arranging extra chairs in a circle.
- having extra Bibles on hand.
- having plenty of Bible study guides and extra pencils.

It is very important to make everyone feel relaxed when you begin your small group meeting.

Step 6: Your meeting agenda

Our small-group agenda arises from Acts 2:41-47. These Bible verses list several items that the early Christian believers did together, including fellowship, prayer, continuing in the apostles' doctrine, ministry, breaking bread together, and meeting the needs of the people. Out of these items arise the small-group agenda, which has three parts—sharing, Bible study, and prayer. Ministry takes place both within the group and during the week.

Sharing time. Give time for members to discuss what has occurred in their personal lives since the previous meeting. Also, use questions that allow the members to get better acquainted with each other—"What is your favorite hobby?" "Where were you born and raised?"

Bible study time. The leader will facilitate the group discussion using the printed Bible study guide.

Prayer time. Ask the group members for prayer requests and pray for them and their needs. Pray for the "open chair," which represents the fact there is room for additional members in the group. Encourage the current members to invite their friends.

When the meeting is over, thank the members for coming and invite them back the next week. Remind them to call you if they are unable to attend the next week, so that the group will not wait for them to come before the meeting begins.

Step 7: Keep the group members returning

- Thank members for coming.
- Make phone calls encouraging members to attend the meeting.
- Get better acquainted. Invite members to lunch or to join you in an activity.
- Have a small-group picnic and do some fun things together.

Step 8: The small group leader's preparation

Set aside time each day for prayer, Bible study, and memorization of Scripture. Remember, ministry is not successful without waiting upon God for the transformational power of the Holy Spirit. Prayer and seeking God's power is the lifeblood of your personal life and of the small-group experience.